Cambridge E

Elements in Business Strategy
edited by
J-C Spender
Rutgers Business School

SCENARIO THINKING

A Historical Evolution of Strategic Foresight

Brad MacKay
University of St Andrews Scotland

Peter McKiernan
University of Strathclyde Scotland

CAMBRIDGE
UNIVERSITY PRESS

CAMBRIDGE
UNIVERSITY PRESS

University Printing House, Cambridge CB2 8BS, United Kingdom

One Liberty Plaza, 20th Floor, New York, NY 10006, USA

477 Williamstown Road, Port Melbourne, VIC 3207, Australia

314–321, 3rd Floor, Plot 3, Splendor Forum, Jasola District Centre, New Delhi – 110025, India

79 Anson Road, #06–04/06, Singapore 079906

Cambridge University Press is part of the University of Cambridge.

It furthers the University's mission by disseminating knowledge in the pursuit of education, learning, and research at the highest international levels of excellence.

www.cambridge.org
Information on this title: www.cambridge.org/9781108469005
DOI: 10.1017/9781108571494

First published 2018

A catalogue record for this publication is available from the British Library.

ISBN 978-1-108-46900-5 Paperback
ISSN 2515-0693 (online)
ISSN 2515-0685 (print)

Scenario Thinking

A Historical Evolution of Strategic Foresight

Elements in Business Strategy

DOI: 10.1017/9781108571494
First published online: September 2018

Brad MacKay
University of St Andrews Scotland

Peter McKiernan
University of Strathclyde Scotland

Abstract: This Element infuses established scenario-planning routines with an exploration of cognitive reasoning, by contextualising scenario thinking within the wider human endeavour of grappling with future uncertainties. Using a study of ancient civilisations, it shows that scenario thinking is not new but has evolved significantly since ancient times. By decoupling scenario thinking from scenario planning, the thesis elevates the role of the former as *the* essential ingredient in managerial foresight projects. The historical theme continues with a focus on the evolution of modern scenario planning, by way of the French and Anglo-American schools of thought, using the intuitive logics methodology. Archival research for the Element has discovered early contributions from the United Kingdom around the development and use of scenario thinking in public policy, which has been overlooked in the many received histories. Finally, the thesis challenges the usefulness of scenario thinking for strategic management and refines the argument that it is simply a heuristic device for overcoming cognitive biases and making better strategic decisions.

Keywords: scenario planning, scenario thinking, foresight, strategic management

ISBN: 9781108469005 (PB), 9781108571494 (OC)
ISSNs: 2515–0693 (online), 2515–0685 (print)

Contents

The range of what we think and do, is limited by what we fail to notice and because we fail to notice that we fail to notice, there is little we can do to change; until we notice how failing to notice shapes our thoughts and deeds.

R. D. Goleman (1996, p. 106), stylised after one of
R. D. Laing's knots (1970)

1 Introduction

Contextual environments facing organisations are often referred to as 'increasingly' complex and dynamic.[1] But it was ever thus. At the macro level, over the past 500 years globally, through the agrarian to the industrial and digital revolutions, contexts have shifted in a perplexing manner. Humanity has struggled with the accompanying changes and, through adaptation, still survived and progressed. Within these periods, the type and nature of the complex and dynamic components alter. For example, within the digital revolution (or post-industrial society), communications transformations, détente in a nuclear age, genetic modification, the countercultural movement of the 1960s, the Vietnam and Cold Wars, the 'white heat of technology'[2] and a series of high-profile political assassinations[3] and their impact on government and governance were pressing issues facing the Commission of the Year 2000, as they challenged intellectual society to think through developments over the next thirty years (Bell & Graubard, 1967). Fast forward fifty years and today's futurists ponder over issues that are arguably of equal puzzlement: diversity and equality, the rise of popularism and nationalism, the impact of technology on work, mass migration, caliphates, terrorism, anaemic Western economies, biodiversity loss, climate change, the rollback of liberal democracies, rogue states and potential thermonuclear warfare. In between, each decade had its ingredients of pressing contextual issues which could be described as complex and dynamic, depending on the perceptions of those doing the seeing and thinking (Marcus, 2009). For instance, in the mid-1990s, Goleman asserted: 'We live at a particularly perilous moment, one in which self-deception is a subject of increasing urgency. The planet itself faces a threat unknown in other times: its utter destruction' (1998, p. 11).

The drama continued at the turn of the century, as Drucker reflected: 'One thing is certain for developed countries – and probably for the entire world: we

---

[1] See, for instance, Ringland, Sparrow and Lustig (2010).

[2] An expression synthesised from a speech delivered by the UK Labour Party leader, Harold Wilson, to the Labour Party Congress in Scarborough in 1964. Wilson actually said: 'The Britain that is going to be forged in the white heat of this revolution will be no place for restrictive practices or for outdated methods on either side of industry.' Wilson went on to become the UK prime minister in 1964.

[3] John Kennedy, Robert Kennedy and Martin Luther King Jr.

face long years of profound changes. The changes are not primarily economic changes. They are changes in demographics, in politics, in society, in philosophy and, above all, in world view' (1999, p. 92). After the global financial crises of the 2000s, drama and turbulence gripped the minds of even the most experienced futurists:

> The uncertainty of the future offers us some near-certainties. Life in large organisations will become ever more complex, time and resource constrained. Competition will become more intense, and scrutiny will be unrelenting. At the same time, the world has seen a financial crisis and faces ongoing changes in the world balance and global systemic challenges. We seem to have reached a number of global tipping points. How can organisations thrive in this environment?
>
> (Ringland et al., 2010, p. 1)

There is no evidence to prove that one generation perceives complexity and dynamism 'increasingly' more than any other. Each has a relative viewpoint that delivers different understandings and feelings. Yet there is little doubt that all contextual environments over time contain a complex mix of components that interact in a dynamic manner and deliver surprise after surprise to everyone, even the most prepared. As the generations pass, it will ever be the case.

Part of the reason for this lies in the vagaries of the human condition. Traditional ways of assisting organisations and governments to navigate the future have rested on the 'predict and prepare' approach of strategic planning (e.g. Ackoff, 1983; Brews & Hunt, 1999), and its use of sophisticated forecasting methods (Makridakis, 1990). Prediction in some areas – e.g. natural systems like climate change – has improved markedly (Ayres, 2000), but society is still surprised by low-probability, high-impact events (Bazerman & Watkins, 2004; Watkins & Bazerman, 2003). The reasons for surprise are likely rooted in the frailties of individual and group cognition and behaviour, which pose a major challenge for understanding the terrain ahead. For instance, at a micro level, these changing contexts are a social construction of individual or group reality[4] and consequently, there are likely many contexts rather than one official one 'out there'.[5] It is this difference in perception and perspective, and the assumptions that underpin them, which makes the future so difficult to predict.

---

[4] Peter Doyle, a leading UK marketing professor in the 1980s–2000s, used to address his first MBA class of the academic year with the assertion that 'perceptions are just reality with a time lag'. Thus, he was throwing the emphasis away from official views of what the market looks like from the supply side, to how consumers think it to be on the demand side. If they see the world as complex and dynamic, then, put simply, it is.

[5] For more explanation, see Lock and Strong (2010).

Even if a single context is assumed, some observers may see it as dynamic and complex while others may see it as relatively simple and stable, depending upon their experience, breadth and depth of vision and psychological make-up, ceteris paribus. A small contextual change to one observer is an indigestible change to another, and vice versa. Hence, environmental complexity and dynamism might be better understood in reference to the lens of the observer and, in organisational contexts, through executives and their composite group vision. Scholars (e.g. Douglas, 1986; Douglas & Wildavsky, 1982) have long posited that different societies, and groups embedded within them, perceive risk and its treatment in different ways, especially when it comes to assessing future dangers. Studying ancient Greek oracular history, Eidinow supports this claim:

> Facing the unchartered future, with all its horrible possibilities, means contemplating the impermanence of stability and prosperity, the inextricable nature of misfortune – and different cultures map this unseen territory differently. Their choice of landmarks turns on their particular world view. The dangers they select as important depend ... on a culturally specific network of beliefs, for example, about the origins of misfortune, their relationships with unseen powers, mortal and supernatural, their understanding of their own capacity to act. (2007, p. 5)

However perceived and by whom, contextual survival and progression require adaptation. Ashby's (1956, 1958) Law of Requisite Variety in cybernetics explains that for an organism to survive change in its environment, it must possess more solutions than the problems it faces. Translating this from the biological to the management sciences, executives and organisations that are not used to change within themselves will struggle to cope when they confront change in their contextual domains. Clearly, any ossification of mental models, or of organisational strategy or structure becomes a harbinger of danger. If these elements become disconnected or 'non-adaptable' to changes in a prevailing context, organisations are said to lack strategic 'fit',[6] and if this is not adjusted, they will embark on a journey of strategic 'drift', rendering future performance unacceptable (Johnson, 1987).

Consequently, executive strategists have to remain in tune with contextual changes and be able to spot the signs of impending future change. Such understanding of uncertainty, and the entrepreneurial ability to adapt strategies to these changing circumstances, are important sources of competitive

---

[6] Whether organisations need to be 'fitted' to their context is a moot point amongst strategists. On the one hand, a perfect fit is impossible and on the other, any fit may lock organisations into a relatively stable platform that induces ossification and thereby restricts enterprise and innovation. Many breakthrough inventions come from the fringe, not these mainstream 'fits'.

advantage. When this does not happen, 'drifting', and possibly eventual demise, are likely to follow (Johnson, 1987; MacKay & Chia, 2013). Hence, non-predictive strategy approaches that embrace contextual uncertainty (e.g. Wiltbank et al., 2006), are likely to herald more success than traditional 'predict and prepare' ones in a world dominated by change and emergence. The most well-known and practised of these is scenario planning.

1.1 What Is Scenario Planning?

Definitions of scenario planning vary to the point of 'rendering it slippery' (Stout, 1998, p. 3). They range from that by Kahn and Wiener, who defined it as 'a hypothetical sequence of events . . . for the purpose of focussing attention on causal processes and decision points' (1967, p. 6), to those by Schoemaker – 'a disciplined methodology for imagining possible futures in which organizational decisions may be played out' (1995, p. 25) – and Godet – 'simply a means to represent a future reality in order to shed light on current action in view of possible desirable futures' (2001, p. 63). The term 'scenario' itself harkens back to the silent film era, when a film script was called a scenario because of its creative, literary and playful connotations (Kleiner, 1996). Building upon these earlier works, we employ the definition from the *International Encyclopedia of Organization Studies*:

> Scenario planning is a process within strategic management that combines the creation of several stories of plausible futures with the practical strategic responses that are required to deal with them. The creation of stories maps the future terrain through a systematic analysis of the key drivers of contextual change.
>
> (McKiernan, 2008, p. 1391)

Organisations adopt scenario planning for a wide range of reasons (Burt & van der Heijden, 2003). Wright et al. (2013) have identified three main purposes: (i) enhancing understanding of causal processes, connections and logical sequences of events that may play a role in shaping the future; (ii) improving strategic decision-making; and (iii) changing mindsets and reframing perceptions in organisations. In our practical work, we find scenario planning used, inter alia, to guide public policy (e.g. the future of regions when oil has run dry), to investigate market entry strategies (e.g. the potential for a new franchise in a foreign market), to enable contentious debate in a neutral space (e.g. between unions and management) and to imagine the outcome of mergers or acquisitions (e.g. on relative share prices and net worth).

While the roots of such scenario thinking can be traced back to the celestial science of the early Babylonians, as a tool for strategic management, scenario planning has continued to increase in use in the private, public and non-for-profit sectors in recent years (Durance & Godet, 2010; Gunn & Williams, 2007; Wright et al., 2016). Finding its modern origins in the work of Herman Kahn and colleagues in the RAND Corporation in the United States in the 1940s, and the work of the French philosophers Gaston Berger and Bertrand de Jouvenel in the 1950s, it proliferated as a tool for planning through think tanks such as the Hudson Institute and the Stanford Research Institute in the United States, and the Association International Futuribles and *La Prospective* in France in the 1960s and 1970s. Early research into scenario planning as a tool for corporate strategy (Klein & Linneman, 1981; Linneman & Klein 1979, 1982 in the United States; and Malaska, 1985; Malaska et al., 1984; Malaska et al., 1985 in Europe) found that just over 22 per cent of large industrial firms in the United States were using the method by the end of the 1970s, and between a third and half of large industrial firms were using the method in Europe by the mid-1980s. Researchers concluded that the adoption of scenario methods was 'associated with the increasing uncertainty and unpredictability of the corporate environment that took place in the 1970s' (Malaska et al., 1984, p. 46). Further, in their annual survey of management tools and trends used by companies globally, Bain and Company documented the steady uptake of scenario planning since their survey began in 1993, gaining momentum after the 9/11 attacks in 2001. It appeared in their top twenty list of management tools and techniques and, by 2015, more than 13,000 respondents from some seventy countries surveyed projected that they would use the technique, making it the fastest-growing management tool (Rigby & Bilodeau, 2015).

With such longevity and widespread adoption, scenario planning has progressed as an essential accompaniment to any prospecting exercise. It has welcomed continuous change within itself; and, this internal dynamism has underpinned its endurance. Perhaps the most significant part of this inherent change is the subtle switch from scenario planning to scenario thinking. Here, the emphasis is placed on the quality of thinking about plausible future terrains and consequent shifts in executive perception, rather than on the more exact science of operational planning that facilitates the negotiation of those particular terrains.[7] For many executives, the challenge is to avoid the blind spots of

---

[7] Mintzberg and colleagues (2008), for example, placed scenarios in the 'planning' school of strategy, rather than the 'learning' school. In earlier work, Mintzberg had emphasised the difficulties that planners have in getting to grips with multiple futures (1994), downplaying notions reported by practitioners that their benefits are in the learning dimensions of challenging cognitive rigidities and helping strategic managers to come to new insights, rather than in planning per se (e.g. De Geus, 1997; Wack, 1985a, 1985b).

not seeing or thinking about potential opportunities or threats by maintaining adaptive cognitive models that keep the organisation in touch with changes in its contextual environment.

Indeed, advocates of scenario planning (MacKay & McKiernan, 2004; Schoemaker, 1995; van der Heijden, 1996; Wack, 1985a, 1985b; Wright et al., 2008) claim that the process of thinking actively about a future contextual state by developing and imagining different scenarios helps generate fresh perceptions, fine-tunes and conditions mental models and informs alternative strategic reactions and timely responses:

> [S]ince the essence of scenario thinking is to examine a range of plausible, alternative futures, the process intervention facilitates ... dissenting opinion ... as to what the future may hold and challenges potentially inappropriate confidence in terms of a single point future and a single, tried and trusted strategy. Simple extrapolations of the past and ... best guesses about the evolving state of *the*[8] external environment are thus attenuated and the degree of alignment between strategy and a range of futures becomes the focus of attention
>
> (Wright et al., 2008, p. 221).

Scenario thinking is a pivotal element of scenario planning – a potent process for challenging mental models through sense making in the presence of confusing signals, through adaptive learning, through the rehearsal of potential crises and through the creation of a strategic conversation between alternate views.

1.2 Contributions and Structure

In sequence, the following sections of this Element are designed to make four main contributions to the Academy. First, we contextualise scenario thinking within the wider human endeavour of grappling with uncertain, unknown and unpredictable futures. Using a study of ancient civilisations, we show that scenario thinking is not new, but it has taken on different forms in different periods of history. Second, we link notions of celestial science with modern-day scenario thinking, demonstrating that the search for greater certainty and rigor in understanding the complexities and uncertainties in the world around us has evolved over time. Third, we decouple scenario thinking from scenario planning and attempt to elevate the role of the former as an essential management support. Fourth, we focus on scenario thinking as it has evolved since the 1940s, by way of the French and Anglo-American schools of thought using the

---

[8] The use of the definite article suggests an environment 'out there' that is given to all and, that is not socially constructed by certain individuals or groups of individuals.

intuitive logics methodology. Based on archival research, we highlight early contributions in Britain around the development and use of scenario thinking in public policy, which has been overlooked in the many received histories in the domain. Finally, we address criticisms over the usefulness of scenario thinking for strategic management and refine the argument that scenario thinking is a heuristic device for overcoming cognitive biases and making better strategic decisions when navigating the complexities and uncertainties of an ever-emerging future. The next section explores this ancient history and illustrates the little-known building blocks of the science of future studies.

2 Ancient Civilisations and Celestial Science

Now, all foresight of phenomena, and power over them depend on knowledge of their sequences, and not upon any notion we may have formed respecting their origin or inmost nature. We foresee a fact or event by means of facts which are signs of it, because experience has shown them to be its antecedents.

J. S. Mill (1865, Part 1, p. 6)

Ancient civilisations have grappled with foresight and prediction to help secure their survival and, to optimise their position with regards to the legitimacy and accumulation of power and wealth of ruling sovereigns. The active pursuit of scenario-based foresight is an ancient practice, having underpinnings that run deep within the ascent of man. Active thinking, analysis and prediction of future-borne threats and opportunities that both endanger survival and promote prosperity, have constantly challenged the intellectual life of civilisations (Cazes, 2008). Because the past is inextricably linked cognitively to our imagining and understanding of potential futures, a study of history is often our sharpest ally during a scenario-thinking or -planning process.[9][10]

In the East, for example, the Chinese I Ching (Book of Changes) was an important source of divination. Using a bundle of sticks, the diviner would

---

[9] This version of history traces the specific legacy of scenario-based foresight. There are other close genres, e.g., science fiction and CLI-FI, that are not covered here because of word limitations, though their influence on scenario thinking is acknowledged. Additionally, many British and Irish authors experimented with future worlds a long time before scenario thinking became formalised in the twentieth century; e.g., Irish author Samuel Madden wrote his *Memoirs of the Twentieth Century* in 1733; English writer Herbert George Wells, who coined the phrase 'foresight' (1932), wrote about what the world would be like in the year 2000, way back in 1901. The anti-utopian writers followed. English philosopher Aldous Huxley wrote his dystopian future *Brave New World* in 1932; English novelist George Orwell wrote his tyrannical novel *Nineteen Eighty Four* in 1949; English sociologist Michael Young wrote the predictive *Rise of Meritocracy 1870–2033* in 1958, written as if it was published in 2034; and the Hungarian/British scientist and Nobel prize winner Dennis Gabor wrote his view of the future in *Mature Society* in 1972.

[10] For a useful contextual, time-line companion to the perceived history interpreted in this section, see Loveridge (2009), chapter 8.

progress through a process of discarding and sorting, creating a hexagram of six unbroken or broken lines, or the Ding. The 'judgement' came first in the text, followed by the image, and comments on each of the lines, supplemented by extensive remarks (Jung, 1989). Also, Sun Tzu, author of the near-mystical treatise *The Art of War*, placed a premium on 'foreknowledge'. Although, he emphasised more terrestrial use of intelligence to understand the enemy, and a careful study of the conditions from which a battle will take place, to develop scenarios for responding to them (Griffith, 1963). Indeed, notions of chaos, flux and uncertainty have long been embedded in Eastern culture (Chiang, 1936; Fang, 1986). For example, such notions are manifest in the two-player board game 'Go', invented more than 2,500 years ago. Where there are some 20 possible opening moves in chess, 'Go' (the name of which translates into the 'encircling game') contains some 361 opening moves, with considerably more possibilities for surprise (Shotwell, 2008).

The analysis of signs and of signals that trigger future events that are familiar to modern-day scenario players was central to generations of Mesopotamian 'celestial scientists', who developed sophisticated foresight technologies long before the arrival of Christendom (Koch-Westenholz, 1995). For example, in the first of all empires, with a history of prescience stemming from the eighth and seventh centuries BC, the Assyrians created an original scenario-thinking mindset, which involved the systematic institutional implementation of foresight for the management and maximisation of the future power and security of the state of Assyria (Rochberg, 2013, p. 1); and, established the importance of foresight as a central strategy for the conduct of imperial business (Rochberg, 2013, p. 3).

Though celestial divination can be traced back to Babylonia in the second millennium BC, the major contributions of Mesopotamian celestial studies have been ascribed two periods in history (Rochberg, 2004). In an early period (circa 2000–1000 BC), 'astral science' embraced celestial divination, horoscopy (not the contemporary form of natal prediction) and magic, in a scribal tradition that can be traced back to Sumero–Akkadian roots. By systematic observation and modelling of the codes of signs in the skies and of natural phenomena, a scholarly body of scientific knowledge was developed and etched into a collection of 'omens' e.g., as in the official compilation of celestial omens – the *Enuma Anu Enlil* (circa 7,000 omens on seventy stones). These were conscious attempts to advise the elites in society of the impact of the stars and the moon on tides, calendars, the planting needs of farmers and, inter alia, the arrival of floods and famines. The Mesopotamians saw star alignments as signs, rather than causes, of physical events: in such omen collections, prognostications, stated as cases in the form *if x occurs, then y will occur*, correlated physical phenomena with events of political, economic or social significance (Rochberg, 2004, p. 3).

Common predictions in the *Enuma Anu Enlil* are at a general rather than a personal level and, focus on primary sector audits around societal survival (e.g. food production, rainfall, flooding) and political-governance issues (e.g. military campaigns, diplomatic relations, destruction of kingdoms). They read like short stories that would be common in contemporary institutional scenario planning e.g. from Tablet 6 (from Rochberg, 2004, p. 76):

> The harvest of the irrigated land will prosper, the land will be happy.
> There will be a scarcity of barley and straw in the land.
> The arable land will prosper.
> There will be rains and floods, the harvest of the land will prosper.
> Downfall of a large army.
> Adad will bring his rains, Ea his floods, king will send messages of
> reconciliation to king. There will be hostilities in the land.

Linked to such divination texts, highly technical texts of astronomy were created that charted star movements and led to practical time-based calendars, and eventually to tide tables. These early heavenly diviners saw the world as a means of communication between man and the gods; where the skies were filled with patterns of divine writings and signals to be read and interpreted, so societal elites could be better informed what the gods had in store. This civilisation accepted 'scientific' observations and divine intervention (or religion) as complementary components of the same whole; for instance, in temple construction, prominent towers were built and used to scan the skies for codes: 'Religion and the foretelling of the future came to be closely associated in men's minds, hence, the large place assigned to prophets and prophecy in the religion of the ancient East' (McClean, 1929, p. 66). Divination was a highly regarded and a legitimate way of predicting the pathway of future events.

The Babylonians made greater progress in mathematical astronomy (as well as the products of the earlier period of celestial divination) in a later period (circa 600–300 BC), exhibiting a technical prowess that the West would recognise now as true science – in design, in process and in outcome. Diaries of the observation of the celestial bodies, as seen in clear skies from the broad Mesopotamian plains, and diaries of political events were accumulated. Personal prognostication emerged through both natal omens (forecasts based upon birth dates under specific astronomical patterning) and horoscope narratives that were built in the absence of personal prediction, with scientific astronomy providing the evidence base. The flow of intellectual scholarship between the Mesopotamian scribal traditions to the latter period of intense mathematical science in astronomy was strong, with evidence that the earlier celestial writings were consulted constantly through the time continuum. This rich Neo-Babylonian (or Chaldean) period was highly impactful, producing the 360-degree circle, the zodiac, the refinement of the sexagesinal system and the twenty-four-hour day.

Historians in the early to mid-twentieth century, consumed by their own definition of 'science', castigated the early period of Babylonian astral science as 'pseudoscience' and viewed the two periods as distinct. However, later historicism (e.g. Oppenheim & Reiner, 1977; Rochberg, 2004) has taken a multivariate interpretation and viewed the elements of the early period, including the role of the gods and magic, as inseparable parts of a coherent mix of a broader scientific approach, with Oppenheim and Reiner (1977) referring to a 'cultural continuum' between these two periods. For instance, in matters of 'celestial science', the Babylonians did not distinguish between 'astrology' and 'astronomy' in the writings of their scribes. Indeed, astrology was a major scholarly pursuit from these early Babylonians in 2000 BC through to the Renaissance in Europe, when it suffered diminution and humiliation at the hands of Newtonian science around the 1680s. Major civilisations (e.g. the Mayans, the Indians and the Chinese) practised the 'science', while it ranked alongside astronomy, meteorology and medicine as a major academic pursuit. From its heartland in Mesopotamia, its spread was accelerated and enriched culturally by the conquests of Alexander the Great; it was mathematically refined and given a personal focus that developed in Grecian foresight, as 'Babylonian culture took possession of Greek thought' (McClean, 1929). Syria, Palestine and Egypt were all influenced profoundly by the Mesopotamian intellectual heritage and the moon zodiac of India and China found its prototype in the twenty-four moon stations found in cuneiform writings.

In Israel's history, the Old Testament preserves a close acquaintance with this celestial science (e.g. Deuteronomy 33:26; Judges 5:20; Exodus 32:15; Psalms 89:11, 77:17ff.), as military advances helped propagate Babylonian culture through Palestine. Though the pantheon of Mesopotamian gods gained a place in the temple of Jerusalem alongside *Jahweh*, Jewish religious leaders remained sceptical of 'the polytheism and formalism of the astrologers' (McClean, 1929).

Beyond the Middle East, the Roman emperors Tiberius and Augustus had court astrologers, as did the English Crown (Edward VI and Elizabeth I). Nostradamus and Galileo advised the Medici, while Kepler advised the Hapsburgs. Astrology is referenced frequently in the creative arts: in poetry

(Gower, Chaucer), in plays (Marlowe, Shakespeare) and in music (Holst). In recent times, Ronald Reagan (through his wife Nancy) had much of his US presidency,[11] including salient talks with Mikhail Gorbachev in Geneva and Reykjavik in 1985 and 1986, guided by the professional astrologer Joan Quigley. As the news of her work broke from the White House in 1988, she told the press that Moses had probably been an astrologer and that Einstein said humans 'dance to a mysterious tune intoned in the distance by an invisible player'.

Expectedly, the shower of criticism against astrology has fallen on the minority contributions of its 'natal predictive' branch, dimming the greater volume and deeper credible heritage of its celestial science. Attacking natal prediction, Cicero used the example of twins born at the same time who could have different traits and trajectories; while St Augustine noted the lack of inclusion and analysis of other potential causal variables (e.g. inherited skills, improved medical care and even better housing) to refute astrological behavioural prediction (see Long, 2005). Helpfully, the mediaeval theologian Isidore of Seville (Wood, 1970) split astrology into two parts: the movement of the stars (including the sun and the moon), which was seen as more scientific and worthy of pursuit, and the prediction of life traits, which was seen as a mistaken field of enquiry.

This troublesome reputation irks modern scientists. Using careful methods, they negate the predictive linkages of this part of received astrology (see, for instance, Hartman et al., 2006; Wyman & Vise, 2008). It seems astrology is no better than chance at forecasting individual behaviour. Modern scientists point to the existence of confirmation bias (a cognitive bias that leads people to recall what turned out right, rather than what was false) that leads astrologers to cling passionately to the subject, no matter what the results or reputation (Nickerson, 1998). Popper (2004) accuses this branch of astrology of not complying with his notion of falsification by experiment, while Kuhn (1970) dismisses the falsification proposition and argues that astrology is not science because the domain is not conducive to research, given its strict conformity to internal governing rules. Thagard (1978) says that astrology is not a science at all, because it has failed to progress by testing and retesting developments to eliminate extant problems and to prospect new dimensions. James and Grim (1982) slam it for its scientific irrationality, peppered as it is with incoherence, lack of credible explanation and inconsistent reasoning. Because astrology is practised in this way and artificially isolated from its deeper roots in

---

[11] Canadian Prime Minister William Lyon MacKenzie King (1921–1926, 1926–1930 and 1935–1948) is also reputed to have relied on the spiritual world – through séances – to guide his political judgement.

mathematics and astronomy, it is easy to find some justice in the pseudoscience claims. But this popular development into horoscopes covers only about one-twelfth of the relevant Mesopotamian chart work (Hansson, 2015), and its critique has blurred the real scientific contribution acknowledged by Isidore.

There is a strong analogy between Mesopotamian celestial science and contemporary scenario planning. Both deal with mastering future uncertainty, and both use 'expert' diviners versed in the interpretation of ominous signs or signals that enable them to facilitate foresightful advice to either kings or chief executives. More, scenario planning can have both a 'pseudo' and a serious side. In many scenario projects, there is a strong process illustrated by a good social science method (e.g. triangulation of data, sampling technique, care with recording and transcribing of interviews, cause-effect modelling and objective facilitation). Additionally, there is a fascination with knowing the future with some precision. The waterfall of criticism that fell on the predictive branch of astrology could be applied to any predictive and probabilistic aspect of scenario planning if predictive power was an important consideration in a futures process. As many experienced scenario planning facilitators know, it is important to accept that scenario planning emphasises how the future *might* turn out, not *how* it will turn out.

As scenario planning creates possible future states, not exact ones, signposts on 'detailed roadmaps' to each scenario are developed that forewarn of the arrival of the possible state. The ancient Mesopotamians built much of their astrological knowledge on such signalling. The observed mathematical arrangement of the stars was related to physical phenomena and explored in omens. 'If x happens, then y will happen' is a mantra used frequently in exploring scenario data sets and building scenarios from them e.g. in soft systems modelling techniques. The predictive narratives etched into the *Enuma Anu Enlil* resemble closely the storytelling, sense making and sense giving of modern institutional scenario planning. Finally, even amidst the critique of predictive astrology, there are believers for whom their belief is both the process and the outcome of a higher meaning than any scientific reasoning or rebuttals. In scenario development, individuals and groups often benefit more from active and committed participation in the process, accepting that the exactitude of an outcome is neither achievable nor of vital importance. This belief is one of the key reasons for owning scenario-informed strategies and engaging more fully with their implementation.

The *Enuma Anu Enlil* was the body of evidence-based knowledge the Mesopotamians compiled to underpin divination, albeit defined by patterns of regularity in the occurrence of natural phenomena. Like scenario planning, these stories were not based upon direct causation, but on analogous combinations of happenings. Yet, despite half a century of practice and in an information-rich, technological world of big data, scenario planning has never made manifest its discovered knowledge of events, trends and drivers and how these might interact and impact under different environmental and cultural contexts. Despite this absence, foresight studies like scenario planning can benefit greatly from Babylonian treatises in a twenty-first-century *Enuma Anu Enlil*. Rochberg (2013) regrets that the lack of continuity of the Mesopotamian heritage into the contemporary era denies us judgement of its influence on social and political reality today. However, the cuneiform stones upon which the celestial science is inscribed are still being translated (only about half of them are in English at the present time). Much cross-fertilisation can occur with both the further pursuit of the legitimate elements of this science that are extant and learning from a mindset that cultivated a sensitivity to external forces, and an approach that attempted to understand rigorously their influence on human affairs.

The scientific method and reputation of the Babylonians in building a knowledge base to underpin their prognosis of future events is a harbinger of modern future studies. Their survival and success depended on the best preparation possible for future surprises that might wreak havoc in their communities. Their legacy was transported widely through military conquests, especially those of Alexander the Great. In the next section, we show how modern scenario thinking emanated from military imaginings of optimum strategies and, how the simulation of those strategies became an essential ingredient of the training of generals in imagining alternative outcomes.

3 A Brief History of Modern Scenario Planning

Forethought we may have, undoubtedly, but not foresight.
    Attributed to N. Bonaparte, French military and political leader, 1769–1821

Want of foresight, unwillingness to act when action would be simple and effective, lack of clear thinking, confusion of counsel until the emergency comes, until self-preservation strikes its jarring gong – these are the features which constitute the endless repetition of history.[12]
    W. S. Churchill, British military and political leader, 1874–1965

3.1 Military Schools of Thought

Conventional knowledge indicates that the modern origins of scenario planning lie in the military and especially in the legacy of the Prussian General Staff (Bradfield et al., 2005; Brown, 1968). Expectedly, military simulation emerges

---

[12] Speech, House of Commons, 2 May 1935.

from war games (Allen, 1987), which have their roots in ancient cultural board games and which, in turn, have their origins in the hunter-gatherer period and the evolution of man's play (Masukawa, 2016). Linking play to fun in the context of a hunter-gatherer society, Huizinga (1955) claims that the skills-based competition represented purposeful play in day-to-day activities more than 50,000 years ago. Like the ancient Sumerians, these civilisations believed their lives to be influenced by the supernatural powers of the gods – as evidenced in early cave paintings of indigenous peoples 35,000 years ago – and made manifest in figurines, believed to represent shamans communicating with the spirit world (Masukawa, 2016). Exploration of the intentions of these gods and spirits was attempted by several means, including extispicy and, with the oracle-based objects like bones and shells (e.g. four-sided astragalus bones from 10,000 years ago). Such bones are found all over the known world of that time and are equivalent to modern-day dice – some dice in Palestine and the Indus Basin have been dated about 3000 BC. Naturally, the dice became the decision tool for simple board games, consisting of moving the bones/shells along rows of squares or in and out of small holes, over which progress was made towards the figurine, sometimes in the presence of 'seers'.

The most ancient of these board games dates back to the Levant in 7000 BC (Simpson, 2007), but other related games (e.g. Mancala) spread across the civilisations in Africa, Cyprus (3000 BC), Egypt (2500 BC) and Mesopotamia and, they can be seen in ancient temple drawings e.g. Abu Simbel (1290–1224 BC). Masukawa (2016) claims that there were four types of board games, significant among them being war games e.g. Chaturanga in India in the seventh century, which is seen as the precursor of chess, and Shogi (Murray, 1952). Importantly, such research reveals much about how our ancestors behaved towards the unknown: exploring the history of board games and game boards involves studying transitions in human wisdom and sensibilities. In other words, such research explores humans through the concept of play, which is indispensable to human life. The history of play is the history of human culture (Masukawa, 2016, p. 11).

Of these games, Chaturanga became the regular game for the army and may have been the first board game to use the language of war in simulation (Murray, 1952).[13] The four 'arms'[14] of the military were present in carved pieces, representing cavalry, infantry, elephants and chariots, which moved

---

[13] The Romans had a board game called Ludus Latrunculorum (Latrunculi for short) from 116 BC to AD 400, which had a civil and a military version. Kings and armies vied to conquer territory over the board as a battlefield. The Celts may have inherited this from the Romans at Hadrian's Wall around AD 200–300 (www.di.fc.ul.pt/~jpn/gv/latrunculi.htm).

[14] *Chatarunga* is Sanskrit for *four arms*.

around the board in a manner similar to modern chess, where these four arms were transposed into knights, pawns, bishops and rooks, respectively. The game spread from India to Persia and onwards to the Muslim world, after the conquest of Persia in AD 651. It had arrived in continental Europe via Spain by the tenth century, evolving in rule and detail and emerging into what is recognisable now as chess, by the fifteenth century (Meri, 2005). Like the game of modern day snooker, chess engages with several foresightful scenarios of the position of the pieces across the board after each future move, including action and reaction of the opposition, as players progress towards a specific end goal. Unlike snooker, it lacks the dynamic human action applied to the cue ball and in particular the possibility of many uncertainties occurring in the process of action (e.g. mistakes by the player taking the shot under pressure, the cue ball 'kicking' badly in an unintended direction due to dust, chalk or problems with the weave in the green baize surface cloth, or the room's environmental conditions affecting the elasticity of the table rubbers).

Variants[15] of chess emerged across Europe, especially the German game of Koenigspiel, invented by Weikhmann in 1664, identifiable as chess, but with a larger board and more pieces. In 1780, Helwig developed the format to a board of 1,666 squares and 200 specialised military pieces, heralding the beginning of modern war gaming. Through the endeavours of Prussian lieutenant von Reisswitz (1824) (Reisswitz & Leeson, 1983), this form developed into Kriegspiel[16] (see later in this volume) and became professionalised as part of the training for the German military. Dropping the formalised chess squares and freeing up movement from the rules-based restrictions of chess, military realism was engineered into the game's play – in what was a paradigm shift for the time. Caffrey (2000) argues that the game may have been responsible for the success enjoyed by the Prussians in the Franco–Prussian conflict of 1870/71. Of the two forms of the game that developed, one was based on rules, the number of which grew rapidly as different situations on the battlefield emerged and, as different regiments adopted different rules for their own play. However, the fundamental rules provided some scientific comfort for the simulations, as they were based on an empirical analysis of actual prior battles. In general, rules-based activity restricts the creativity of thought that inspires improvisation – a key success factor in military operations. Contrarily, the other form of the game encouraged a freer thinking mode. The interpretation of the rules was left to human umpires who could adjudge a particular situation or outcome as

---

[15] This section draws upon material from the war game website at www.faculty.virginia.edu /setear/students/wargames/page1a.htm, https://en.wikipedia.org/wiki/Military_simulation and von Hilgers (2012).

[16] *Kriegsspiel* is the German for *war game*.

they saw it. This science of human judgement was not always verifiable because of the variability between umpires in the decision-making process, so rendering prediction from the simulation difficult.

In this era, the development of board-based war games is inextricably linked to the changing face of warfare itself. For instance, European warfare in the eighteenth century was determined and limited economically and politically by the capabilities of the states of absolute monarchs (Goerlitz, 1953), who either claimed supreme power by divine right (especially in Russia) or saw themselves as the first servant of the state (Prussia). Their highly trained, professional armies were expensive to maintain, difficult to replace and technically excellent, though mechanistic:

> Infantry marched right into the battle line in firm, mathematically circumscribed formations. It fought in lines three deep, several sets of triple alignments drawn up one behind another. All evolutions were carried out according to rule, with the soldiers in all their ingenious wheeling and manoeuvring keeping strictly in step. The aim was the welding together of the men so that they moved and fired with the synchrony of a single machine ... The strategy of the time was that of a chess board.
>
> (Goerlitz, 1953, pp. 6–7)

Though warfare might have been a matter of mathematical precision, much depended on the ingenuity of the monarch who led the troops. In Prussia, though the inspirational Frederick the Great brought success (e.g. in the three Silesian Wars and the Thirty Years' War – 1740–1763), the record of his immediate successors was not strong. The monarchy had become large and cumbersome and the need arose for a greater supporting bureaucracy and a bigger role for a professional elite, who could both plan for war and support it. In 1787, the Supreme War Council was formed, led by field marshals who reorganised affairs into three units responsible for mobilisation and provisions, uniforms and equipment, and the disabled (Goerlitz, 1953). Though the traditional Prussian army had become the model for other European armies, its old model was in the process of reform with the transfer of power from monarchs to a professional military elite, laying the foundation for the infamous Prussian (later German) General Staff. Established by law in 1814, its formality and necessity had been triggered by Napoleon's defeat of the Prussian army at the Battle of Jena in 1806. The legacies of the Industrial Revolution and the Enlightenment had combined to alter both the refinement of weaponry and the attitude to monarchical favour or wealth, respectively. Hence, the Prussian 'Great' General Staff recruited intelligent officers from a new variety of backgrounds. Trained to exceptional levels and proven on the field of battle, these 'elites' had a lifelong loyalty to the corps. Ironically, they were still led by those appointed through patronage, prompting one of them to remark that their task was to 'support incompetent Generals, providing the talents that might otherwise be wanting among leaders and commanders' (Gerhard Scharnhorst, quoted in Boot, 2006, p. 122).

Scharnhorst, Von Clauswitz, Von Krauseneck, Von Schlieffen, Von Hindenburg and Von Moltke (the Elder) were influential members of the General Staff. The latter, versed in Clausewitz's moral and political writings embedded in his famous treatise 'On War' in 1832, recruited only the cream of graduates from the Prussian Officer Training College (Kriegakademie) and trained them personally in all theoretical and practical aspects of warfare, including simulations using Kriegsspiel – see earlier in this Element (McElwee, 1974). Many military forces borrowed this German technology of war gaming to train officers, fortify war plans and simulate strategy e.g. the Greeks, the Rumanians, the Turks and, even the French under General Miribel in 1871 and, later, the United States in 1898.[17] Von Moltke thought the unthinkable in warfare, departing from both the sombre practice of the eighteenth century where the 'purpose of war was the avoidance of war' and the prior dominant Prussian thinking that war was only possible to win on a single front. Scenarios were developed for the east, south and west of Prussia, with multiple contingencies – even to the point that when Prussian strength reached a specific level, a war fought against both France (west) and Russia (east), on two fronts, might be possible to win (Kitchen, 1975).

Much of this military 'scenario' thinking influenced the eventual Von Schlieffen Plan (the German Strategy for World War I) many decades before it was developed fully (Ehlert et al., 2014). A disciple of the German General Staff College, Von Schlieffen held annual winter war games from 1896 to 1905 – the only complete one to survive is from 1905 (thirty-six pages with seventeen maps). It begins thus:

> The situation on which this war game is based is the same that appeared months ago in the *France militaire* and later the *Matin*, from which it was picked up by all the newspapers. It concerned war between Germany on the one side and England, France and Russia on the other. As unlikely, or better yet, impossible that such a war will ever take place, it offers enough interest to us to concern ourselves with it. For about 20 years, we have lived in the expectation of war on two fronts. It has been said again and again for 40 years

---

[17] Walter Millis, writing the introduction to Goerlitz's 1953 book, claims that the United States turned to the German General Staff College in 1898, for example, when it decided to modernise its military system.

that in addition to a theatre of war in the east and one in the west a third in the north would be added.

(Von Schlieffen, 1905, p. 1, in Zuber, 2004, p. 167)

Despite the depth of thought and rehearsal embedded in the final Von Schlieffen Plan, it stalled on impact with reality. The modern machine gun helped switch the advantage in warfare from attack to defence. Consequently, the Belgians (through whose neutral territory the attack traversed) could defend vigorously and, together with poor weather, delayed the action that Von Schlieffen demanded to take Paris in a stretched target of twenty-eight days. This allowed the British (signatories to the Palmerstonian[18] penned treaty on Belgium's neutrality) sufficient time to mobilise, reinforce the defences and prevent the Germans from reaching Paris in the number of days planned. Arguably, the detail within the plan may have been a reflection of the mechanistic chess playing that dominated warfare before the emergence of the German General Staff (see, for instance, Tuchman, 1966) as the inherent inflexibility in the plan contributed to its downfall. Clearly, scenario thinking that covered multiple eventualities was probably considered by Von Schlieffen, but rejected in favour of a single, fast *blitzkrieg*.

The legacy that modern scenario planning owes to the German General Staff[19] is large. In turn, the Staff owed much to the embodiment of war gaming in its training and, much of this was premised upon ancient games rooted in the world of gods and spirits, shamans and seers of the ancient civilisations. Modern military thinking, from analytical models and computer simulations to major field exercises, grew out of this heritage. Indeed, the RAND (meaning research and development) Corporation, along with MIT, specialised in both manual and sophisticated computer-simulation models of military-political scenarios for the US Pentagon and armed forces, especially during the Cold War. The depth of experience garnered by RAND influenced the development of commercially orientated scenario-planning processes like intuitive logics (see Section 3.5), that are used widely today. But this military heritage has overshadowed the legacy in the European theatre, where the Babylonian–Greco influence on Western society was strong. The spread of Christianity across the Continent through the Roman Church, brought the inevitable clash between God and man over who has the final say on future happenings. The next section draws upon this legacy and

---

[18] Lord Palmerston was the British foreign secretary who signed the Belgium treaty of neutrality.

[19] Despite being banned under the Treaty of Versailles in 1919 and Hitler's preference for the Oberkammando Wehrmacht, the German General Staff never really disappeared until Germany's army was disbanded at the end of World War II. Note that there was serious rivalry between the two groups (e.g. in the 1944 Valkyrie plot).

shows how the Jesuits influenced the development of a powerful French school of future thought.

3.2 The Emergence of the French School of Thought

Mesopotamian celestial science had a significant influence on world cultures, especially Greek political thought, which, in turn, fuelled the intellectual development of Western civilisation. Oracular institutions grew up across Greece from the fifteenth century BC and lasted until the fourth century AD. Of the forty-nine oracular sites (Curnow, 2004) that included Dodona, Ammon and Didyma, the most famous was in the Temple of Apollo at Delphi. But, as Eidinow (2007) notes, it would be foolish to think that they all operated in the same manner in trying to resolve the pressing foresight concerns of politicians and other significant members of society.

In Israel, Assyrian influence was reflected in the passages of the Old Testament before the dawn of Christianity. The emergence of Christianity and the New Testament pronounced the 'infallibility' of divine providence that dominated the early spread of the Roman Church throughout Europe. Arguably, formal European futures thinking can be linked to the sixteenth-century revival of Scholasticism, triggered in part by the Catholic reaction at the Council of Trent to the Protestant Reformation and, in particular, to the creation of the Jesuits' 'ordering of daily life' after the death of their founder, Ignatius Loyola, in 1556.

Loyola prepared his fraternity to practise their faith through guidelines specified in his *Constitutions*, which became enshrined in rules, shaped by the powerful hand of the Jesuits' Father, General Acquaviva. Decreeing that Jesuit education should be based on the works of St Thomas Aquinas and Aristotle, Acquaviva aimed to show that: the data of science and enquiries into nature could be harmonised with the data of faith (Martin, 1988, p. 202). Consequently, Jesuit scholarship flourished in a golden age during his regime. Preeminent among their intellects was the Spanish theologian Luis de Molina, who played a central role in one of the most tumultuous intramural doctrinal disputes in Catholic intellectual history (Freddoso, 1988, p. 5). Molina's thirty-year cogitation resulted in his 'lumbering' and controversial treatise on grace and free will – *Concordia* (1588). This 'Middle Knowledge' lens presented a reconciliation of man's free will with God's foreknowledge of future events, grace, divine providence and predestination through 'conditional future contingents' or 'futuribilia' (Malaska & Virtanen, 2005). Countering the broadly held notion that it is God who controls the acceptance of grace, Molina defended free will by asserting that humans can choose whether or not to accept that grace. He was not proposing new ideas but laboriously sorting and, carefully restating, very traditional ones (Mitchell, 1980, p. 128). An extract from Ecclesiasticus (15:16–18) illustrates man's choice and the belief in God's complete foresight:

> He has set fire and water before you;
> put out your hand to whichever you prefer.
> Man has life and death before him;
> whichever a man likes better will be given him.
> For vast is the wisdom of the Lord;
> He is almighty and all-seeing.

Immediately, Molina's thesis drew the wrath of the Dominicans, who rejected it as lacking a direct derivation from the teachings of their spiritual guide, Aquinas (in his *Summa Theologica*). He had asserted that humans have no freedom to accept grace unless God permits it. The fierce intellectual dispute that followed had to be silenced by decree on the intervention of Pope Paul V in 1607, long before a clear victor emerged. This argument still rages in the Church today, but Molina's theological thinking and concepts lived on in twentieth-century futures studies (see later in this Element).

Molina would recognise how the gods featured foremost – at least as power-fully as royalty – in Mesopotamian culture and its imagined futures. In particular, the evolutionary tussle between God and man over divine foresight – where human culture interpreted the signals of the gods through natural phenomena on the earth and in the sky – would be strikingly familiar. Rochberg notes that:

> This all-important feature of foresight in cuneiform culture is the distant cousin to our own English usage meaning Providence, or Divine Foresight. Contrary to Western assumptions about the inevitability of Divine Providence, sometimes associated with the natural order of the world itself, ancient Near Eastern gods were amenable to prayer and ritual appeasement, as evidenced in the many extant prayers and apotropaic rituals against evil portents from such things as the appearance of animals, snakes, malformed births, and lunar eclipses.
>
> (Rochberg, 2013, p. 4)

In France after World War II, Molina's treatise was resurrected in a different context and for a different purpose by the philosopher Bertrand de Jouvenal (see later in this Element), one of four early influential pioneers who shaped French futures thinking. Rebuilding whole economies after the war meant that long-term thinking was imperative. France became a pioneer in weaving scenario-based thinking around deep futures into its political, economic and social development. The early French futures landscape was entwined with the concept of *La Prospective*, as developed by the philosopher, industrialist and politician Gaston Berger (1964); he created the Centre Universitaire International et des Centres de Prospective in Paris, and launched the journal *Prospective* in 1957. Famous for his dictum 'the purpose of the future is to disturb the present,' he was dismayed by the strictures of quantitative futures techniques e.g. probabilistic forecasting. Berger provided a context and humanity to both the past and the present happenings, and thus facilitated a different kind of exploration of multiple deep futures to aid current French political decision-making. Godet points out that:

> The inadequacy of 'classical' forecasting techniques can be explained by their downplaying, or outright ignoring, of the role played by creative human actions in determining the future. This creative attitude is recognized by the 'prospective' approach, which reflects awareness of a future that is both deterministic and free, both passively suffered and actively willed.
>
> (Godet, 1982, p. 295)

Berger's *La Prospective* approach embraced the actions and spirit of humans in shaping multiple possible future outcomes. Importantly, he assumed it possible for humans to model different futures and take actions to build their preferred choice. This proactive creation, or the bringing about of a desired future, contrasts markedly in philosophical terms with the (forecasting) notion of the future as an extrapolation of the past to a single point end, and with alternative philosophies that underpin some of the thinking amongst competing approaches e.g. the intuitive logic disciples (see, for instance, Wright and Cairns [2011], whose future assumption is a more reactive one). Importantly and crucially, the approach placed emphasis on the understanding of uncertainty rather than on the elements of predetermination – a feature common to other scenario-thinking approaches, including intuitive logics (see Section 4), but notably absent from comparative tabulations of contemporary scenario methods (see, for instance, Amer et al., 2013, p. 28; Bradfield et al., 2005, p. 808).

Bernard de Jouvenel, who had joined the Prospectives Centre in 1966, and Pierre Masse developed Berger's work throughout the 1960s. Masse directed the fourth of France's five-year plans from 1960 to 1965 and was instrumental in the fifth (1965–1970), embedding scenario thinking within them (de Jouvenel, 1964; Gordon & Glenn, 1994). But, it was de Jouvenal who developed Molina's term 'futuribilia' by combining the words 'future' and 'possible' to form 'futuribles' – meaning a 'fan of possible futures' (de Jouvenel, 1967, 1972). Funded by the Ford Foundation, de Jouvenal brought together twenty international intellectuals of different disciplinary backgrounds and founded the group Futuribles in 1960.[20] The Futuribles published extensively on futures affairs throughout the early part of the 1960s (more than eighty futures essays were written between 1960 and 1964) – a process that De Jouvenel (1964) claims was to garner a forward-looking habit within society. He wanted to open up French minds to futures beyond those determined by a minority elite towards broader people-focussed opportunities (de Jouvenel, 1967).

Stressing the need to accept that the past and the present are already complete and to focus explicitly upon the future, he addressed the RAND Corporation in 1964:

> [L]ead me to assert most vigorously: 'There is no science of the future.' The future is not the realm of the 'true of the false' but the realm of the 'possibles'. But while there can be no science of the future, we cannot avoid thinking about the future. We do so implicitly: it is better to do so explicitly.
>
> (de Jouvenel, 1964, p. 2)

This speech was significant in introducing many 'intuitive logics'–influenced scenario thinkers to the different Futuribles approach and vice versa. Clearly, there was much intellectual cross-fertilisation, as we see in what follows, with American, French and British engagement with future thought, evident in the Commission for the Year 2000 in 1965. The chairman, Daniel Bell, was well connected to the Futuribles and another Futurible, Michael Poznan, a professor at Cambridge University, sat on the Commission alongside RAND and Hudson Institute scenario supremo Herman Kahn. The work of Michael Young and Mark Abram, who were instrumental in the British Social Science Research Council's Committee on the Next Thirty Years project – whose interest lay in identifying those areas of social science most needed over that time frame – was well known to Daniel Bell. Additionally, de Jouvenel gave advice to their Committee both in person and in writing during the mid-1960s (Mark Abram's private files, Churchill College Cambridge).

The original Futuribles organisation metamorphosed into the Futuribles International Association, first under de Jouvenal and then under Pierre Masse. Well-funded from government sources, it eventually brought all the French foresight houses into one home, including Berger's Centre Universitaire International et des Centres de Prospective. Despite these French connections, it was not solely nationally focussed, having prepared studies on the future of other countries like Spain and Burma. Originally, it functioned as both a repository of foresight publications and a catalyst for bringing top international thinkers together, but later, it served as a consultancy for foresight studies. It remains one of the world's premier foresight stables.

---

[20] See www.futuribles.com/en/qui-sommes-nous.

In the 1970s, Michel Godet further developed Berger's pioneering method *La Prospective* (as refined by de Jouvenel). Godet agreed with the general approach of Berger's process in terms of multiple futures – the outcome of the actions and reactions of human actors, and the exploration of causal paths from the present to the future. He departed from the overt simplicity of mere pictures or stories: literary scenarios, however, although they may represent a stimulating exercise for the imagination, suffer from a lack of credibility. It is impossible to verify the validity and plausibility of the hypotheses advanced (Godet, 1982, p. 298).

In response, he infused scenario thinking and building with the harder 'science' of computer modelling and statistical analysis, introducing a series of software programs (MICMAC, MACTOR, MULTIPOL, MORPHOL and SMIC). Briefly, through cross-matrix analysis, MICMAC allows the impact of one variable on another to be assessed, while MACTOR analyses the ways in which human actors converge or diverge in their thinking over key issues. MULTIPOL helps generate and sift through strategic options. MORPHOL is the application of morphological analysis – a way of systematically reducing a problem to its individual parts and searching for a maximum number of re-combinations of the parts, while SMIC is a cross-impact probability method that helps identify the most plausible scenarios and other combinations of hypotheses that could have been omitted otherwise. Often, this form of scenario building entails the use of the Delphi technique and embraces the use of forecasting where it would add value:

> Although quantification at any price may seem dangerous, the numerical results of 'classical' forecasting models (time series econometric) do provide stimulating indicators and valuable reference points for a consideration of the future. We believe that there is a certain complementarity between the 'prospective'; and the 'classical' forecasting.
>
> (Godet, 1982, p. 300).

For Godet (2001), this strategic scenario building was a necessary component of scenario planning. Clearly, as Bradfield et al. (2005) point out, the *La Prospective* (LP) approach contains much that is familiar to the intuitive logics (IL) process, but its computational techniques can mask human interaction and human intuition, rendering it more of 'a blend of the intuitive logics and probabilistic trend methodologies' (p. 803). However, the same authors argue (after van Vught, 1987) that the principal difference between the two processes is that the early IL work was mainly global, and the early LP work was mainly French. Both de Jouvenel (1964) and Godet (1982) would dispute this assertion, claiming that much of their earlier work was international as well as French, quoting far-reaching essays and discourse on many non-French proprietary topics and on the use of the *Prospectives* methods in many Latin countries, including South America. Whatever the debate and despite the power of the American publishing machine behind the IL process (see Section 3.5), the French 'school' has made an impressive and lasting contribution to prospective thinking. However, few scenario planners can escape the ubiquitous presence of the RAND-shaped American school of future thought.

In the next section, we illustrate its influence and introduce the mind-stretching 'intuitive logics' approach that emerged as the dominant scenario approach.

3.3 The Emergence of the American and British Schools of Thought

Arguably, corporate futures studies in the United States date from the 1930s, with President Hoover's Research Committee on Social Trends (1930–1933) and the publications of the eminent sociologist William Ogburn (chair of the Committee), on social and technological trends and future prospecting (1933, 1934, 1935). Hinting at the corporate engagement with futures work, Ogburn proclaimed that: "To understand social change, it is important to know how inventions are made and diffused" (1933, p. 331). However, Schoemaker (1993) argues that the root of modern scenario work goes back to the use of computer simulations by atomic physicists of the Manhattan Project in 1942.[21] There is no question that the intensity of such studies accelerated after World War II, when technological advances in weaponry outstripped military planning activity, often neutralising its effectiveness. The US secretary of state for war, General H. H. Arnold, saw the need to formalise and consolidate the wartime teamwork of scientists, industrialists, military professionals and politicians in a post-war environment, so the US armed forces would be future-proofed for the planning and development of new technologies.

A private organisation called RAND was set up in association with the Douglas Aircraft Company. Its first report in 1946, entitled 'Preliminary Design of an Experimental World-Circling Spaceship', indicated the direction of its intellectual travel, while other early studies, couched in the onset of the Cold War, defined its 'futures' pathway e.g. 'Towards New Horizons' by (1945) and the RAND project on international conflicts (1948) – see Builder (1996). Carl Builder, a defence analyst at RAND for more than twenty-seven

---

[21] For example, Lawrence, Teller, Compton, Oppenheimer.

years, notes that: 'Perhaps the highest aspiration of the joint venture that initiated RAND was to explore the frontiers of knowledge. Thinking "outside the box" – or daring to think imaginatively – has been a consistent feature of RAND throughout its 50-year association with the Air Force' (Builder, 1996, p. 11). RAND ideas shocked the US air force commanders in the 1970s, as they imagined what were to become modern-day drones – aeroplanes without pilots. The cross-fertilisation of experts coupled with the use of the latest technology enabled RAND researchers to develop most of the practical weaponry of modern futures work e.g., Delphi studies, systems analysis and scenario-planning methodology.[22]

Though scenario thinking and planning owe much of their origins to the military, their transition to the commercial world stems mainly from the initiative of Hermann Kahn[23] during the 1950s and 1960s, as a strategist at both the RAND Corporation and the Hudson Institute (Kahn, 1960, 1962). Kahn's unconventional thinking penetrated very sensitive arenas, where he thought the 'unthinkable' about topics such as the roll-out of a nuclear war and the consequent rise in birth defects, contaminated food and growth in cancers and even how such a war might be won.[24] The character Dr Strangelove (or, 'how I learned to stop worrying and love the bomb'), played by multipart British actor Peter Sellers in the 1964 film of the same name, is partly based on Kahn (Kleiner, 1996). At RAND, his technique of writing a postcard from the future to be read today translated these imaginative stories as 'scenarios'[25] – part of a process that he called 'future-now thinking'. Solutions to complex economic, social and political issues arising in these scenarios stretched the computing power of the time, so RAND built one of the first mainframe computers with stored memory in 1948.[26] Such computational capacity facilitated the development and application of game theory and military war game

---

[22] RAND continues to provide objective and rigorous research for the public good with more than 1,750 employees in forty-nine countries (www.rand.org/about.html).

[23] Though Kahn's work at RAND and Hudson has propelled him to a status as the 'father' of scenario planning, Berger's work in France developed in parallel, though each had different triggers – the former with military assertiveness in mind and the latter to achieve a broader public benefit. The power of Anglo-American publishing and media may have promoted Kahn's work to this preeminent state, perhaps (unfairly) relegating Berger's powerful contribution into second place.

[24] Kahn's book *On Thermonuclear Warfare* was eventually published in 1960, delayed due to security classification.

[25] Originally a term in theatre referring to 'a sketch or outline of the plot of a play, ballet or novel etc., with details of scenes and situations' (Shorter Oxford English Dictionary, Clarendon Press, Oxford, 1993).

[26] It was named JONIAC after child prodigy in mathematics and game theory genius John von Neumann.

simulation scenarios, including the development of scenarios for the US Air Defence early warning system in the 1950s at RAND (Schoemaker, 1993).

In 1961, Kahn founded the Hudson Institute with Max Singer and Oscar Ruebhausen. Its purpose was 'to think about the future in unconventional ways'.[27] Here, Kahn applied his RAND scenario knowledge to issues of social and public policy, stretching the public's imagination to deep futures through extensive publications, especially the Year 2000 project with Anthony Wiener in 1967.[28] Using a combination of three futures techniques (trend analysis, event clustering in thirty-three-year frames and statistical projection), Kahn and Wiener (1967) created scenarios around 'a "standard world" and several "canonical variations"'. Under science and technology assumptions, they imagined many developments that are familiar to consumers more than fifty years later. Inter alia, they included:

- Multiple applications of lasers
- Super-high-strength/temperature materials
- Super-performance fabrics like plastics
- VTOL aircraft and supersonic jets
- Fuel cell propulsion and nuclear-powered electricity grids
- Substitutions for human organs
- Robotic production lines.

Raubitscek (1988) claims that this work of Kahn and Wiener did much to forge the scenario planning field because it both defined and framed scenarios within the strategy firmament; proved its capability in exploring and making sense of complex and uncertain environments for policy purposes; exported the futures techniques more widely than before, and generated significant reaction in published works[29] – thus put scenario thinking and planning on the strategic map. Kahn's other colleagues at RAND – Olaf Helmer, Norman Dalkey, Bernie Brown, Theodore Gordon and Wendell Brown – all helped to spread the word in both corporate and social projects. For instance, Helmer and Gordon helped found the RAND spin-off – the Institute for the Future (IFTF) in 1968, with ambitions to develop the national scenarios for the United States, amongst other early initiatives (Helmer, 1972). Dalkey and colleagues at the Stanford Research Institute (SRI) made the transition from their experience in mostly public-centred scenarios for societal change to developing scenario planning for the commercial sector. This foresightful imperialism spread two 'branded' but related approaches – intuitive logics and probabilistic modified trends –

---

[27] www.hudson.org/about/history
[28] For access to this early work, see Bell and Graubard (1967), pp. 73–100.
[29] See, for instance, the Club of Rome Reports.

globally over the next fifteen years,[30] while Kahn's ideas about the unconventional happenings in deeper futures attracted the interests of several major corporates, who became part of the sponsorship programme at Hudson. These included Corning, IBM, General Motors and oil and gas giants Exxon and Shell. Taken by Kahn's alternative future thinking, Shell's planning analyst, Edward Newland, started to persuade colleagues of the value of scenario planning.

Shell was to become a global powerhouse in scenario thinking, spawning consultancies across the globe. In London, its planning executives shared a strong intellectual interest in embracing the uncertainty that future prospecting demanded. Their engagement with cutting edge British academic scholarship in the decades after World War II, enriched their approach to scenario thinking.

The British have a long heritage in academic and practical prospecting e.g. the work of Emery and Trist (1965) at the Tavistock Institute on the typology of organisational environments. Like RAND, the Institute grew from actions during World War II, when its forerunner, the Tavistock Clinic, performed psychiatric work with the British army. This psychological and sociological experience gained it many friends amongst large companies during the 1950s and 1960s e.g. Shell, Unilever, Bayer and Glacier Metals. Tavistock played a major role for the newborn Social Science Research Council (SSRC) in 1965. On its inception, the Council set up six subject-based committees (e.g. economics) and a seventh Committee on the Next Thirty Years (NTY). Its purpose was to prepare reports speculating on the prospective future demand for social science research from the perspective of actual and potential users. The Committee was led by Michael Young, the SSRC's chairman, who had a history as a sociological futurologist (see Young, 1958). The NTY worked closely with other visionary organisations with parallel projects at that time (e.g. ICI for the Year 2000 and Unilever for the Year 1984; the RAND corporation on the Ford Foundation project Resources for the Future; the Commission for the Year 2000 project; the French Committee on the Year 1985; de Jouvenel's Futuribles; UNESCO's study on 'Future Trends in Social Work' (which had Tavistock input); and the European Cultural Foundation on its Plan Europe 2000 project[31]).

---

[30] Linneman and Klein (1983) claim that more than 50 per cent of companies in the Fortune 500 listing were using the technique by 1982.

[31] The Foundation was launched in 1968 and had four futures projects: 1) Educating managers for the twenty-first century; 2) Social sciences and the future of industrial man; 3) Urbanisation – planning human environments in Europe; 4) Rural societies in the year 2000. NTY had a presence at its 1970 conference on 'Citizens and Cities in the Year 2000', which was part of the urbanisation initiative.

In the beginning, the NTY's main concern was the driving force of technology on pressing social science issues (Abrams, 1966)[32]:

- The gap between elite knowledge and public knowledge
- Unemployment and its effect on participatory decision-making
- Poverty and social welfare provision
- Management–union relations in the context of nationalisation
- Increasing urban concentration
- Market stratifications by age and the socialisation of young people
- The reconfiguration of government units
- Training, motivation and guiding of the labour force

To handle the range of issues, the NTY needed both stakeholder support and learned futures research. Thus, it engaged with the Confederation of British Industry (CBI), the Trades' Unions Congress (TUC) and a variety of government ministries. It commissioned futures reports from a variety of bodies on retirement pensions (Ministry of Pensions), international organisations, industry (CBI), food consumption (Office of Public Health), war studies (Institute for Strategic Studies), consumption (Unilever), mass media (Redifussion), industrial enterprise (Chatham House), local government (Institute for Operational Research) and decision-making (Emory and Twist at Tavistock).

There is evidence that scenario thinking and writing (imported mainly from RAND but informed by de Jouvenel), coupled with the Delphi technique, contextual mapping and time series analysis, were used in some futures studies by the SSRC e.g. the 'Future of the Social Sciences' by Eric Twist of Tavistock (1968, p. 52). This is against a background when trend analysis was largely conducted through the statistical progression of econometrics. The debate of quantitative over qualitative prospecting that faced de Jouvenel and Godet in France and, later, Shell in the late 1960s and early 1970s was fought earlier in the United Kingdom in the NTY projects. At a conference organised by the ICI and the RAND corporation in May/June 1966, Abrams (1966) noted the stark difference in futures outlook between a) scientists and technologists and b) scientists and social scientists. Perhaps because the SSRC and NTY teams had a strong sociological background and presence, qualitative techniques like scenario writing became more acceptable, especially when coupled diplomatically with time series analysis. Strangely, this early use of scenarios in social planning

---

[32] Eminent UK social scientist Mark Abrams was secretary to the Initial NTY Committee. His papers are archived at Churchill College Cambridge, and this reference is from a handwritten note in his 1966 files.

in the United Kingdom has been little noticed. The main thrust of scenario planning history has been received powerfully, both academically and practically, down a DNA lineage from Kahn at Hudson and RAND and through the Shell Corporation's missionaries like Newlands, Collins and Wack (see later in this volume). Clearly, other historic stones need to be overturned as this little known British presence that influenced a generation or more of social projects and became the forerunner to many government foresight projects (see, for instance, www.gov .uk/government/collections/foresight-projects) in the decades that followed.

France, America and Britain all contributed unique facets of modern scenario thinking. Of course, these are not the only schools of thought, but they have become the most influential. In the next section, we compare the French and Anglo-American contributions – the two schools that have dominated scenario planning to date.

3.4 Comparing the French and Anglo-American Schools of Thought

Both the French and Anglo-American schools experimented with techniques that combined quantitative and qualitative approaches. Further, there was much interaction between the schools in their development. In particular, two probability-based futures techniques – cross-impact analysis (CIA) and trend impact analysis (TIA)[33] – were developed at RAND and IFTF by Helmer and Gordon (see earlier in this volume) that incorporated human judgement in the detection of transformational events that would render the single-point estimates of traditional forecasts neutral. These are known as probabilistic modified trends because they involved modifying the statistical algorithms of the extrapolation software to incorporate probabilities from human judgement. Over the years, many computer simulation models have been developed around the CIA, including BASICS (Battelle) and INTERAX (University of California). Indeed, the cross-fertilisation between the French and American schools continued as Godet (with Duperrin) developed their own cross-impact software (SMIC) for prospecting in France, (Gordon & Glenn, 1994). Unlike IL, and despite the extent of the mathematical modelling involved, the variation in approach and software is minimal while the link to TIA through human expert judgement via the use of another RAND product (Delphi), remains very strong.

In the academic scenario world, there is some debate as to how many approaches to scenario planning exist. For example, Huss and Honton (1987) identify three major ones (TIA, CIA and IL) and four scenario analysis

---

[33] See appendix 1 for a fuller description of these techniques.

techniques (SRI, Futures Group, BASICS and INTERAX), while Bradfield et al. (2005) advocate three major categories or schools (IL, *La Prospective* [LP] and probabilistic modified trends [PMT]). The latter approach has some logic as a) the former authors do not register the *La Prospective* school at all, and b) there is such a common root (see earlier in this Element) between both TIA and CIA that they can be classified together as a product set – though they have a mirror in the software tools used in LP (e.g. MICMAC and SMIC). The three approaches from the latter study are illustrated in Table 2, in the appendix.

The main similarities between them surround the project horizon – where each has a deep futures orientation, and both focus around a specific problem or issue of importance to the sponsoring organisation. Though, the PMT approach requires access to reliable time series data, which can restrict it when the problem or issue is a softer, qualitative one e.g. human resources management issues in corporations. The largest differences are between the qualitative IL school and the quantitative PMT school, which is ironic, given their common RAND stable. Indeed, IL shares much more with the LP approach, which is strange, given they evolved quasi independently, though with some cross-fertility (see earlier in this Element).

The main differences between the approaches are fivefold. First, IL has a broad utility scope and has been especially useful for a) sense making in complex and dynamic contexts, whether internal or external to the sponsoring organisation; b) future prospecting, anticipation and sign posting, particularly where major capital investments are being considered; c) strategy and policy formulation; and d) organisation and individual learning, where mindset change is a necessary partner of a strong scenario process. Perhaps because LP and PMT integrate more computer software whose computer iterations shield people from engagement, the major mindset alterations among executives and managers occur in an effective IL process (see later in this Element). Second, knowledge generation in IL is largely subjective, although some objective material may be involved in confirming assumptions during deliberations. In both LP and PMT, the approach is steered more towards objective views of a reality through an externally directed process. Once again, humans can be isolated from activity under such assumptions and mindset changes become less likely. Third, in an IL process, people within the sponsoring organisation are encouraged to own the process and so are engaged fully at the centre of it, with the support of a facilitator. Such projects fail regularly if this facilitation is not experienced, sensitive and expert (see, for example, Hodgkinson & Wright, 2002). Alternatively, in both LP and PMT, external experts drive the process with their proprietary and sophisticated software – to which few internal organisational people have either access or knowledge. PMT may be more robotic than LP in this regard. Fifthly, IL demands that each scenario is equally probable while both LP and PMT provide probabilities for their range of scenarios. Finally, the IL output is part of the creativity of the process and is shaped by narrative – stories, song, plays or poetry. Frequently, photography, video imaging, photo montage and even computer gaming are used to enhance the presentation. Both LP and PMT share a highly quantitative, analytical output with minimum narrative.

Most of the academic literature has focussed on the IL approach. Its qualitative nature has found an easy home in organisations dealing with seemingly intractable issues that people wish to embrace and understand. A plethora of consultants and 'how to' books have created both a widespread IL use and a proliferation of short-form methods and techniques within it. Some of these have little resemblance to the original form developed at RAND and the Hudson Institute and commercialised by the Shell organisation. This is understandable, as a comprehensive scenario project is expensive and can take months or years to complete, while many organisations need a quick fix in the present.[34] Nonetheless, the transparency of the IL process (soundly facilitated) means that organisational actors engaged within it can see their own future pathway evolving and can begin to live in the scenarios developed. This engagement allows an easier ownership of any consequent strategy and policy and for many, grants permission to think about intangible issues in a plausible way.

Unlike PMT and to some extent LP, IL is a people process wherein current and future cognitive perceptions, changes and stimuli are of central concern. Minds accustomed to long periods of limited change can find change more difficult than minds accustomed to fast-moving contexts which, in turn, can find long-term thinking unimaginable. The role of human cognition in thinking about deep futures is the engine of the IL process and yet much of its happenings and interaction with differing contexts remain a mystery to scenario planners. We explore this phenomenon in the next section.

4 The Intuitive Logics Process

Albert Einstein called the intuitive or metaphoric mind a sacred gift. He added that the rational mind was a faithful servant. It is paradoxical that in the context of modern life we have begun to worship the servant and defile the divine.

R. Samples (1976, p. 26)

---

[34] Though much business for expert scenario facilitators comes from rectifying in-house (DIY) scenario projects that have stalled.

In envisioning multiple futures, the underpinning philosophy inherent in Kahn's thinking became known as 'intuitive logics' (IL) – a combination of instinctive feel and judgement around future happenings and a logical consistency of cause and effects that might lead to them. Thus, scenarios became plausible to humans assessing their own, constructed futures and 'scientifically' acceptable to a discriminating community. Here, the 'two cultures'[35] of art and science combine synergistically in the interrogation of uncertainty. The early corporate acceptance of scenario thinking and planning ran against the grain of practised futures technology, as planning was akin to a formal science in the board rooms of the 1960s and, for many, well into the 1970s. Large-scale, long-term planning models, which were in vogue for both governments (especially in Europe, as it rebuilt after World War II) and organisations (e.g. corporate planning and then strategic planning), influenced future prospecting and organisational direction. Major plans with detailed objectives spanning at least five, if not ten years, with precisely quantified financial flows, accompanied by detailed implementation actions (the Von Schlieffen plan is a close analogy), and complex control mechanisms were developed for, and by, large corporations – see, for example, the classic texts of Argenti (1968, 1974) and Steiner (1979). Improved mainframe computer power made the technical projection and control characteristics of the plans possible and so helped spread their usage to a broader corporate constituency. For instance, throughout the 1960s, oil and gas giant Royal Dutch Shell[36] relied upon a comprehensive computer-driven, quantitative cost and sales forecasting model – the Unified Planning Machinery (UPM). Its discipline permeated the organisation and brought precision to the short-run (six-year) financial forecasting. The UPM dominated the culture of the organisation though, ironically, as Wilkinson and Kupers (2014) note, 'even within the (*six year*) horizon, UPM tended to get a lot wrong.'

However, many of Shell's strategic decisions in the oil and gas sector demanded knowledge of much longer futures (e.g. more than twenty-eight years for the life of an oil refinery, and decades for large tanker fleet investments), especially in regard to the oil price itself. In 1967, Newland criticised the UPM for its short six-year horizon, which he claimed was not stretched enough to capture the roll-out of impactful trends in the sector, and argued for Kahn's longer scenario approach. But, as de Jouvenel (1967) and Godet (1987) found in

---

[35] In a manner unexpected by C. P. Snow (see, for example, his 1959 REDE Lectures).

[36] Hereafter, references to Shell refer to the Royal Dutch Shell Group of companies and its central services in London and The Hague, not the Shell Oil Company in the United States. A more detailed history of these early years in Shell can be found in Wilkinson and Kupers (2014, chapter II, pp. 25–74).

France, this qualitative approach was a major intellectual challenge to the elaborate quantitative frameworks of forecasting and, in Shell's case, the numbers-driven UPM culture (Kleiner, 1996). Its introduction and acceptance faced a multitude of deep-rooted psychological and behavioural problems. Thankfully, key influencers like Victor Rothschild (research coordinator) and Jim Davidson (head of planning) became early product champions (Patel, 2016).

Between 1967 and 1969, Shell, through Ted Newland[37] and Neville Beale, experimented with narrative-based, deep future thinking in the Year 2000[38] project that examined the business context, some thirty-three years hence. Concluding that there would be a hiatus in projections before 1985 due to major discontinuity in the sector and knowing that the formal forecasting model in the UPM would fail when faced with discontinuity, Shell invited several of its companies to look to 1985 from 1969 through a 'Horizon Year Planning (HYP)' (Wack, 1985a) exercise. The head of planning for Shell Française, Pierre Wack,[39] used France as an experiment for the new scenario thinking tools as the country contained two critical uncertainties that made it ideal for a technique designed to embrace them – the availability of natural gas and the championing of national companies. The experience allowed Wack and colleagues to sort out the predetermined elements (those events that have happened and whose consequences are not known) and critical uncertainties and to generate four first-generation[40] scenarios. Though the exercise provided few new ideas, Wack (1985a) noted that it did uncover a pretty useful planning tool to challenge the UPM.

The HYP project confirmed the results of the Year 2000 project with the B[41] family scenarios challenging the assumptions of plentiful and cheap oil that had dominated Shell's forward thinking in the UPM. The first-generation set was developed into a second-generation set after examination of the individual

---

[37] Kahn had warned Newlands about the consequences of 'business as usual thinking' that the likes of the UPM might furbish.

[38] The end of a 1,000-year period is engrained in ancient religions as one in which transformational things occur e.g. in early Christianity, chiliasm (Greek = 1,000) marked the 1,000-year earthly reign of Jesus while the Book of Revelation (20) talks of a second coming of Christ (Parousia) and a judgement day after a 1,000-year reign. In the 1960s, many projects stared ahead to the year 2000 e.g. the Commission for the Year 2000 (see Bell & Graubard, 1967) and the United Kingdom's Social Science Research Council's Committee on the Next Thirty Years led by council chair Michael Young with Cambridge scholar Mark Abrams in 1967. TV documentaries and press special issues (e.g. *Time* magazine and the *Wall Street Journal*) popularised the magical year also.

[39] Like Newlands, Wack had prior meetings with Kahn.

[40] First-generation scenarios are a starter group of stories that await fuller investigation through data input and analysis, and so develop into the second-generation or decision scenarios.

[41] The Shell planners developed A family (business as usual) scenarios and B family (challenge the status quo) scenarios.

behaviour of the oil-producing states. Some of the new scenarios advocated the restriction of oil supply in the Gulf States and the concomitant supplier (OPEC) reaction in raising oil prices, thus reversing the agency power between oil companies and oil-producing countries to a sellers' market. These were presented to executive management in the autumn of 1972. True to form, OPEC's oil price rises arrived, not as precisely as argued in the scenario, but as a reaction to the foreign policy of the United States during the Yom Kippur War in 1973. The 400 per cent increases in 1974 shocked the oil-dependent Western world, wreaking havoc on production, market competition, transportation and national inflation. Scenario planning had enabled Shell to prepare for the rise (if not its timing) and, consequently, it moved from the number eight oil company in the world to number two (Willmore, 2001). After the Iran–Iraq War in 1981, the company could sell off excess oil reserves as its competitors continued to stockpile, and before prices collapsed (Wack, 1985a).

Scenario planning had helped Shell executives to achieve an understanding of the future that the UPM could never have done, given its mathematical strictures. This success enabled the scenario experiment to progress in Shell. In 1972, this was done alongside the UPM, in a limited part of the organisation, to handle conservative opinions and then, in 1973, it was spread across the group. Afterwards, the UPM was dismantled. But, initial take-up of the scenario approach within the group was slow. Many managers saw the 1972 scenarios as of great intellectual interest but something that did not spark action, despite the warnings of impending doom in the sector. Wack and colleagues realised the need to develop a 1973 set of scenarios whose task was to both inform and shift the global mindsets of these managers away from the status quo towards a new reality. The UPM's legacy was deeply psychological. The new scenarios both broke the existing view and, through increased managerial engagement, helped build the new one.

In group planning, Davidson, Newland, Wack, Napier Collins and others developed and refined the technique at Shell. After differing levels of success, scenario planning through IL prospecting[42] became the root of Shell's planning approach. Wack is credited as the major influence and stressed the 'knowing' and 'seeing' components of the process. Selin observed that: 'The practice of scenario planning is characterised here as populated by *professional dreamers*, capturing both the rational and esoteric elements of the practice' (2007, p. 11). This embracement of both predetermined and uncertain elements defined Shell's approach to modern scenario planning. Its acolytes spread the technique across the globe, both in consultancies e.g. Peter Schwartz (1991) and Napier Collins

---

[42] Sometimes affectionately, if erroneously, known as the 'Shell approach'.

(Global Business Network, California) and, in academia e.g. Pierre Wack (Harvard Business School in 1984), Gareth Price and Brian Marsh (University of St Andrews Scotland in 1988); and Kees van der Heijden (University of Strathclyde, Scotland in 1991). Today, the organisation[43] remains one of the major exponents of, and most quoted examples for, generic scenario development and its application. Embodied in its process is an ambition to preserve a broad decision-making space through an embracement of a leadership and culture that embodies dynamic learning and innovation. The core principles of this process, developed over fifty years, provide the bedrock of the culture. These are illustrated in Table 1.

The IL scenario-planning process pioneered by Shell is explained extensively elsewhere (e.g. Amer et al., 2013; Chermack, 2011; Ringland, 2002a, 2002b; Schoemaker, 1993; van der Heijden, 1996; van der Heijden et al., 2002). There are so many variants in methodological approaches that some authors have referred to a methodological chaos (Martelli, 2001) and others claim that there is a method for each practising consultant (Bradfield et al., 2005). This flexibility is essential because of the greatly differing contexts facing organisations, the content of the future issues under examination, the nature of the resources available and the political attributes and agency dispersal of internal cultures.

Briefly and generically, the process contains a number of stages from project scoping and diagnosis of the issue under study, including the setting of boundary conditions like the sector, the geographical region and the time horizon for the end scenarios (five, ten, fifteen, twenty years or more); data collection through single and group interviews (which may incorporate the Delphi technique) with key stakeholders, technical experts and exceptional people and through extant publications, including archival investigation; database building; data analysis using soft systems modelling, forecasting of predetermined variables and content analysis of the narrative material; the synthesis of analysis; exploration of the key emerging issues through expert opinion; scenario building with all engaged stakeholders; scenario writing; scenario testing for plausibility, internal consistency, comprehensiveness, surprise, inter alia; scenario refining; and scenarios of strategy and policy, including the building of signposts and pathways to these futures (see Figure 1). These stages are linked together tightly, and the process is non-linear, having many feedback loops that allow the learning and thinking to feedback into prior stages, so improving quality, exposition and erudition.

---

[43] In its examination of extant scenario processes, the Hart-Rudman Commission (1999) claimed that 85 per cent of the scenario studies it examined could be traced to the Shell process.

The process is an ingenious mix of art and science. Ideas generation, unconventional thinking, novelty, surprise, causal and quantitative modelling and artful facilitation point to a creative process (Poincare, 1913; Weisberg, 1993) that provides powerful insights into how the future might unfold and what actions executive teams can take now so that organisations might survive and thrive. Not all is positive, as inherent in such processes are the seeds of destruction that can negate all the creative work if they are not handled properly e.g. process failure and lack of buy-in (Hodgkinson & Wright, 2002), job dissatisfaction (Zhou & George, 2001), dislikes of innovative behaviour and destructive conflict (Janssen, 2003, 2004) and simple discontent (Livingstone et al., 1997; Miron et al., 2004). But despite its weaknesses, 'intuitive logics' scenario planning has sustained a presence among national and organisational planning techniques for more than fifty years – well beyond the fashionable management fad (Abrahamson, 1991; Gill & Whittle, 1993).

Of all the approaches to scenario planning, the intuitive logics one involves more of the human element in imagination, shaping, exploring and deciding. Yet, we argue, the notion of scenario planning needs to be decoupled from that of scenario thinking to emphasise the importance of the cognitive elements that underpin the intuitive logics process. We turn to this in the following section.

5 From Scenario Planning to Scenario Thinking

> There is something I don't know that I am supposed to know. I don't know what it is I don't know, and yet am supposed to know, and I feel I look stupid if I seem not to know it and not know *what* it is I don't know. Therefore I pretend I know it.
>
> R. D. Laing (1970, p. 56)

5.1 Scenario Thinking

Thinking about the future can consume undue cognitive space in the unconditioned mind. Few executives and fewer managers have the time to ponder unknown events and what the future might hold. Thus, what they can know and what they don't know can act to constrain their thinking. The busy milieu of organisational life made heavy with bulging in-boxes, stubborn KPIs and short-term thinking can hinder future prospecting and generate minds focussed mainly on targets and efficiency gains – doing things right. Effectiveness, or doing the right thing, becomes a poor relation. Countless corporate examples tell of a failure to detect dangerous threats because of such unidirectional thought and its associated repetitive actions. One of Shell's original scenario architects, Pierre Wack, noted long *before* the global financial crisis (GFC) of 2007/2008:

In times of rapid change, a crisis of perception (that is, the inability to see an emergent novel reality by being locked inside obsolete assumptions), often causes strategic failure, particularly in large, well-run companies. Problems resulted from a crisis of perception rather than from poor strategic reasoning. These decision maker's strategies made sense and indeed were often brilliant – within a context of their limited worldview.

(Wack, 1985a, p. 150)

The lessons from the GFC, when toxic trading incapacitated the global economy for more than a decade, emphasised the need for continuing organisational vigilance in thought and action. Before the crisis, the thought patterns of many financial traders seemingly 'failed to notice' that the continuous selling of loans to people who could not repay them[44] hinged upon the basis of ever-increasing property prices – a dangerous assumption in any era. Such thinking tends to focus on what is already known, assumed or can be known, so reinforcing a belief in how we think things will turn out.

The problem of making inductive inferences based on received data, experiences and observations has been successively referred to by Hume (2007/1748), Mill (1973/1865), Popper (2002/1959) and, most recently, Taleb (2007) as the inductive problem of 'black swans'. The black swan *problematique* refers to the empirical dilemma where the mere sighting of a large number of white swans does not 'justify the conclusion that all swans are white' (Popper, 2002, p. 4), but that the very sighting of a single black one is sufficient to refute the claim that 'all swans are white.' For Taleb (2007, p. xvii), who has recently popularised the notion of 'black swans', they reflect events that are outliers that carry extreme impact, and that cause individuals, companies and indeed governments to 'concoct explanations for [their] occurrence after the fact making [them] explainable and predictable'. Black swans represent the unthinkable 'otherness'; the 'what could have but did not happen' way of thinking about goings-on in the world (MacKay & Chia, 2013, p. 211).

This thinking pattern frequently results in 'blind spots' when analysing the future, and suboptimal strategic decisions, and ranks high amongst many reasons why overt signs of catastrophe are not detected (Zajac & Bazerman, 1991). As scholars pointed out after the terrorist attacks of 9/11, the signs of impending crisis often lie all around us, yet we still don't see them. Fortunately, there are ways to spot danger before it is too late (cf. Bazerman & Watkins, 2003, p. 73). Besides political and organisational concerns, these scholars claim that much of the blame for this blindness is down to a raft of executive and managerial cognitive biases – like overt optimism about present positions,

---

[44] The clue was the term 'subprime'.

gross subjectivity in data analysis, love of the status quo and de-sensitivity from the abject problems of others.

Good future prospecting relies on rectifying these mental constraints, spotting signals early and thinking through their likely ramifications. Yet, while the future cannot be known, training in thinking about its different shapes and forms allows it to be better understood. True, its complexity and dynamism can mesmerise mindsets, rendering ineffective orthodox 'business as usual' thinking and its related strategy making. A short-term, operationally focussed thinking is limited in this pursuit. Long-range, scenario-based foresight requires that mindsets shift from this singular bounded thought into the challenge of thinking from multiple perspectives about multiple futures – stretching existing thinking. A clearer cognisance of the underlying historical and contemporary forces of change and how they might shape a variety of plausible future states or scenarios forms an integral part of this foresight process.

Such a cognitive shift sharpens imagination and develops a deeper comprehension of what might lie ahead. By embracing rather than ignoring uncertainty, prospective scenario thinking allows individuals and organisations to make better strategic decisions today. By exploring a range of scenarios and thinking through their likely individual impact on the organisation, strategy making can benefit from future-proofing. By constantly considering the early warning signs of future happenings, thought is focussed around the particular future emerging and any necessary reactions to it. By engaging in dialogue about the forces of change and their likely future outcomes, a singular perspective can be broadened and developed in the face of counterpoint and debate.[45] Finally, by generating strategic reactions to future scenarios in advance, early response can be implemented that might lift performance and secure longevity.

The actionable parts of such scenario thinking can be seen in the game of snooker, where players vie to 'pot' alternate red and coloured balls with a white 'cue' ball, building 'breaks' by amassing points in the process. Whether active or non-active[46] during a game, professional players constantly assess the position of the balls. Before attempting a 'pot', the active player will translate this visioning into how they will try and build a 'break' to amass as many points as possible. Clearly, their *optimistic future* is to pot all the balls and maximise the points accrued (147), while their *pessimistic future* is to miss the first pot

---

[45] As in a Hegelian dialectic.

[46] Players take turns at the 'potting' during the game. Active players cede position to non-active players when they fail to make a 'pot' or commit a foul. In particular, scenario thinking can be seen when peering into the face of the non-active player as they study the array of balls and the shot(s) played by the active player. The execution of this thinking or its manifestation in a plan can be seen in the study of the actions of the active player, when observers can see the skill being applied.

and hand the advantage over to their competitor 'on a plate'. It may transpire that a maximum is not technically possible because of the position of the balls and so they might have to settle for a *satisficing future* that maximises the number of possible points in their break and then leaves the 'cue' ball in a secure (or ideally in a snooker) position to minimise the competitor advantage. To build their optimistic future, top players survey the balls in front of them and then think multiple shots ahead – how the first pot leads to the second to the third etc.; hence they have to imagine what the layout of the balls is after each of these shots before they take their first shot – a scenario view of multiple futures. All the time, they remain 'vigilant' about the position of their 'cue' ball, trying to imagine a relatively safe layout should they miss a particular pot, such that their opponent could not cause them too much damage. Without this long-term future thinking ability coupled with immediate defensive routines in the present, ordinary players can only hope that they 'pot' the ball confronting them and possibly the one after that. For the skilful player, long-term scenario thinking around multiple plausible outcomes and its planning counterpart are alive in the game.

Hence, scenario thinking can be defined as *a cognitive process concerned with imagining how the future might unfold in multiple ways through the analysis and judgement of the effects of the actions and reactions of shaping forces*. Pure scenario thinking involves thinking about the future and its range of possible states with or without action, or any codified planning technique. Pragmatically, Lindgren and Bandhold (2009) hold to a set of principles that underpin their own perception of scenario thinking (see Table 1):

Table 1 Seven Principles of Scenario Thinking

1.	Acquire a Toolbox (Analytical techniques, interviewing, systems modelling)
2.	Handle Your Brain with Care (Balancing energy used with the rest required)
3.	Think in Dramas (Who? What? When? Where? How? Why?)
4.	Think in Futures (What leads to what, and when?)
5.	Think in Uncertainties (Avoiding predictable space and dysfunctional change)
6.	Think in Systems (Dependencies, interdependencies, events-trends-structures)
7.	Think in Actors and Moves (Understanding the actions of stakeholders involved)

Source: Adapted from Lindgren and Bandhold (2009)

The snooker players rehearse most of these principles of scenario thinking before they take a single shot. They isolate their thinking from their doing (or shot execution). Yet once they commit to a shot, they begin to enact their plan. The next section follows suit in decoupling thinking from doing in the scenario process.

5.2 Scenario Planning

Often, scenario thinking is coupled to scenario planning. Perhaps because of the variety of methods[47] and different historical beginnings, precise definitions of the latter have escaped scholarly reason (Bradfield et al., 2005; Godet, 1990; Godet & Roubelat, 1996; Mason, 1994; Simpson, 1992). Moreover, it has been suggested that as many multiple definitions (e.g. strategic scenario building versus scenario planning) are used interchangeably, it seems irrelevant to exclude any at this point (Varum & Melo, 2010, p. 356). Here, we deliberately decouple thinking from planning in the manner of Wright and Cairns (2011, p. 4). Their expert treatise begins by encouraging such a divorce, and then linking the two in a detailed exposition of the most popular scenario-planning method (intuitive logics), so emphasising both the independent operation of the two and their planning productivity in combination. As Martelli (2001) suggests, because scenario planning cannot exist without scenario thinking or scenario building, the latter are the 'necessary foundations' of the scenario-planning process.

The decoupling of scenario thinking from planning activity allows a cognitive approach to future prospecting to become an active, practised mental process. Thinking happens and the consequential plan is developed and enacted, but the thinking never stops, despite the progress of the plan. Moreover, thinking thrives upon individual and group creativity in organisations, where it relies on the human ingredients of intuition and emotion as futures become socially constructed realities. As the agency moves from actor to actor in a group dialectic, the power play involved shapes thinking and action. Strategically, the coupling of thinking and planning becomes a strong learning loop, reinforced by experience – especially of failure – and so enhances future prospecting.

Scenario planning is used extensively in public institutions and corporate organisations to understand the range and types of uncertainty associated with future environmental contexts (Linneman & Klein, 1983; Pagani, 2009;

---

[47] Scenario methods have a dynamic development record, with new versions being created through theory and practice-led improvements (see, for example, Technology and Social Forecasting Special Issue [80/4 May 2013], edited by G. Wright, G. Cairns and R. Bradfield).

Ringland 2002a, 2002b; Schoemaker 1991, 1995; van der Heijden et al., 2002). Significantly, this process allows executives and managers to reflect on their existing thinking and to stretch that thinking into the uncertain and unpredictable, but understandable deep futures. Deep futures are time horizons that are well beyond what they may be used to in their day-to-day operational activities (Schwartz, 1991; Wack, 1985a, 1985b; van der Heijden, 1996). Then, after opening up of minds to both the mundane 'obvious' and the surprising 'unthinkable', more effective and creative organisational responses become possible and the plan can be developed and enacted.

In scenario planning, prospective thinking is captured in a set of rich descriptive narratives or stories that are illustrated often with artistic media e.g. photographic collage, poetry, paintings, film and so on. These stories tell the tale of how the imagined world evolved and portray the detail of life in the potential end states. In some scenario-planning processes (e.g. intuitive logics – see Section 4), because the intention is not to predict a single future, stories are used to show a variety of plausible futures based on a detailed analysis of the driving forces e.g. economic, environmental, political, social, technological, that emerge from the past, that act on the present and that influence the future. Essentially, it is a genre (de Geus, 1997; Fahey & Randall, 1998; Wilkinson & Kupers, 2014) that communicates understanding and meaning of competing futures in an unthreatening manner. Much prospective and reflective thought occurs within a scenario-planning process, especially if the process is linked to soft systems thinking (Checkland, 1981), where an armature of logical, non-linear maps links causes to outcomes and forms a respectable science base that can lend credibility to both the cognitive process and, especially, a belief in generated scenarios. Purposively, this prospective thinking culminates in the construction of multiple futures and these are then related to planning as a strategy or policy reaction, for example, in interpreting the meaning of each future by way of threats or opportunities for the organisation. Strategies can be prioritised to attack and/or defend, and goals, policies and actions brought together to tackle the issues inferred from the scenarios. Scenarios have been used successfully by Royal Dutch Shell to anticipate the oil shocks of the 1970s (Wack, 1985a, 1985b) and the impact of the collapse of the Soviet Union on gas prices in the 1980s (Schwartz, 1991); by South Africa to chart a peaceful post-apartheid future for the country in the 1990s (Wilkinson & Kupers, 2014, pp. 55–56); and by Apple to understand the future of 'digital lifestyle', and to shift into the mobile phone industry (Hartung, 2009).

However, the scenario approach to strategic foresight has attracted a good deal of criticism. As Schoemaker (1993, p. 2) has long noted, the gist of the scenario method seems that it is many things: art and science, deduction and induction, structured and fluid, rational and political. These multiple facets have caused it to remain elusive and fuzzy by academic standards.

Essentially, scenario planning's roots in practice mean that the usual academic underpinnings of theoretical rigour and academic legitimacy claimed by other futures processes, with roots in mathematics and statistics (e.g. probabilistic modelling, real options theory), are limited (Goodwin & Wright, 2001). Despite these frailties, scenario planning is an integral part of strategy practice and discourse (Cummings & Daellenbach, 2009). Focussed and growing academic research over thirty years (see, for instance, Varum & Melo, 2010) and widespread practice over the past four decades have enabled it to sustain a presence amongst management techniques significantly longer than the ubiquitous management fad. It seems destined to enhance the strategic management toolbox for years to come.

One reason for its endurance is its interplay with other foresightful tools and techniques for making sense of the future. This armoury for enhancing foresight is voluminous and sophisticated, containing both qualitative techniques (ranging from extispicy within celestial divination, through storytelling and on to scenario thinking and planning) that embrace human judgement visibly and quantitative techniques (ranging from simple regression point forecasts to multivariate analysis of big data) that render this judgement relatively invisible. The latter tools can privilege the known over the unknown in their preference, for instance, for predetermined variables over uncertainty. Their future predictions are generated from computational algorithms hidden within statistical software and their results presented within probabilistic confidence intervals. On the one hand, by minimising human interaction, these techniques can reduce the transparency and executive ownership of consequent futures state(s) and any strategic reaction to them. On the other, the notion of quantitative inspired accuracy can trick the mind, with the mathematics and statistics persuading us of the legitimate work of powerful science. Drucker (1999) argues that executives are so seduced by the rapid internal data analysis of computers, that they often ignore or fail to find time to study issues generated on the outside of their organisation. Yet, as he emphasises, normally, major change stems from *outside* the firm, not from the inside.

Hence, credulous executive acceptance of the outcomes can arrive relatively easily. Despite this dilemma, machine-generated forecasts can be accurate over a short time period, until the point whereby the value of their assumptions begins to dissipate. Despite such limitations, quantitative modelling can be integrated with human judgement in a scenario process with long-term scenario thinking being reinforced by multivariate forecasting, especially over the short term, to produce a plausible and a logically consistent set of future scenarios.

Through thinking – planning – action, organisations can complete the learning loop that underwrites a strong process of strategic foresight. Provided scenario thinking never stops once the plan is enacted, executives can build upon what they know, improve the range of what they can know and assess better what they don't know. This analysis of the signals[48] of impending future change and its illustration of plausible futures is a modern version of foresight, which has a mirror in ancient history (see Section 2). We explore the challenge of such scenario thinking in the next section.

6 Scenario Thinking: The Cognitive Challenge

> Nothing in life is to be feared, it is only to be understood. Now is the time to understand more, so that we may fear less.
>
> M. Curie (quoted in Bernard, 1973, p. v)

6.1 Perception and Cognition in Strategic Management

Over time, strategists have tried to explain why some executives and their teams fail either in this contextual adaptation or in foresightful prospection.[49] Understandably, the reason seems to lie prominently in faulty cognitive systems or processing, especially when these are rooted and stuck in the past (Barr et al., 1992; Mackay & McKiernan, 2010). But, as Grinyer, Mayes and McKiernan (1988) emphasise, organisational stagnation measured by relative performance decline is not due solely to misaligned cognitive models. It is more likely to be the result of multiple causes, some of which are external to the organisation e.g. unforeseeable changes in demand. However, their finding on cognitive models and associated thinking patterns is telling:

> A particularly difficult situation occurs where a substantial track record of past success reinforces patterns of judgement which are no longer appropriate in changed circumstances and enhances the credibility and power of the combined chief executive and chairman, not only bolstering *his* belief in *his* own ability to handle the evolving situation in ways familiar to *him*, but also making *him* unchallengeable until the failure becomes very clear indeed and possibly dramatic.
>
> (Grinyer et al., 1988, p. 28)

Such circumstances reflect what Wilensky (1967, p. 121) has referred to as 'the conditions that foster the failure of foresight'. These conditions have been shown consistently to include multiple information management and

---

[48] Stemming from pioneering work by Igor Ansoff (1975), weak signals play a key role in strategic foresight and in scenario planning in particular (see Seidl, 2004, for an insightful reflection)

[49] This argument is founded and developed from material in MacKay (2009) and McKiernan (2017).

processing difficulties, the tendency to minimise the importance of emergent changes in environments, distracting 'red-herring' phenomena and rigidities in individual and institutional beliefs, which culminate in a 'cultural collapse' and an absence of the prudence deemed adequate within the organisation when coping with uncertainty (Turner, 1976, p. 380). This view is supported by Miller and Freisen (1980), who tell of the suppression of alternative views that threaten the status quo through the use of strong political pressure in organisations. Often, dissenting managers, or information that challenges dominant managerial or organisational logics, can be side-lined or dismissed.

In these circumstances, the process of decline can spiral around a dominant mental model, as executives try to solve salient problems through its existing lens and hang onto this lens as long as possible. This process can have four stages. First, relatively poor performance can be ignored as executives enter denial on the basis that it is a short-term phenomenon and recovery is just around the corner. Continued decline might see denial switched to blame, as isolated organisational incidents carry the burden of cause e.g. a major IT failure. Whatever the narrative, the existing cognitive model remains. Second, if relative performance continues to decline, costs (especially advertising and training – both of which are technically investments) are cut and the resultant performance is appraised. If it is acceptable, then the organisation can continue to run within the same cognitive model and its associated 'way of doing things'. Third, if decline persists, then portfolio rationalisation e.g. cutting the range of products or services, may be attempted. If this works, then executives are able to hang onto the original cognitive model. Fourth, if the latter strategic action fails, the organisation may be left teetering on the brink of disaster. Survival will depend on considerable triggering to shock the entrenched thinking. This is likely to require a heavy external intervention e.g. from financial institutions or shareholders. Often, executives (especially the CEO) gripped by the original cognitive model will need to be replaced by others who can introduce new ways of thinking and better sense external signals, translating these into appropriate action.

6.2 The Cognitive Challenge

Scholars (Wright et al., 2008) have attempted to explain this cognitive inertia by reference to the decision-making ideas within the conflict theory proposed by Janis and Mann (1979). This theory notes human behavioural responses to coping with contextual challenges and explains how some of these create far more executive stress than others, especially where severe losses (including their own posts) might occur. Executives develop 'coping patterns', depending upon the amount of stress perceived. In low-stress contexts, there is time to search for more information and take action (*vigilance*); there is no threat to change the current action (*unconflicted adherence*); and in *unconflicted change*, the current action can be switched to another that is unthreatened. In higher-stress contexts, executives know that they have little time to search for a solution that they know exists (*hypervigilance*). When they perceive that 'no solution exists other than the current one,' *defensive avoidance* occurs in one or all of these three ways: by decision delaying, by passing the decision onto others to make and by stressing the benefits, and minimising the criticism, of the current solution.

Goleman (1998) links this type of perceptual behaviour to the brain's capacity to absorb pain by masking its sting, but at the cost of diminished awareness. This coping mechanism can be translated from an individual's character to group interaction and broader society. In each of these domains, the variety of 'pain' blocked from awareness is successively refined, from stress and anxiety, to painful secrets, to threatening or embarrassing facts of social life (Goleman, 1998, p. 22).

Research in cognitive neuroscience (e.g. Li et al., 2016; Warren et al., 2016) suggests that effective decision-making processes rest on the ability of people to convert past experiences into accurate predictions about the likelihood that a desired outcome can be realised and, identifying when past experience is rendered irrelevant due to changes in the external environment. Understanding the meaning of uncertainties arising from unexpected events, and what neuroscientists refer to as the 'learning rate', is critical to this task (e.g. Behrens et al., 2007; Nassar et al., 2010; Nassar et al., 2012). For example, unexpected events often result in stock market fluctuations. Stock market investors must learn to identify when values have dipped temporarily or permanently to avoid selling too soon or too late. This necessitates balancing adaptation to changes in the environment and drawing on observations to refine existing beliefs about the stability of their environment.

While cognitive systems have been shown to adjust the learning rate to volatility in the external environment, neuroscientists have also shown that cognitive systems will allocate attention to, particularly, initial events, often missing events that follow on in close succession. They refer to this as the 'attentional blink' (e.g. Broadbent, 1958; Broadbent & Broadbent, 1987; also see Baskin-Sommers et al., 2012; Warren & Holroyd, 2012; Wolf et al., 2011), or 'inattentional blindness' (Posner & Rothbart, 2007). The import of the attentional blink for the strategic management of organisations is that attention shapes perception by identifying the information that managers focus on, which is either dismissed or missed altogether (cf. Kosslyn & Rosenberg, 2006; Simons & Chabris, 1999).

Under stress, the brain has developed ways of coping, which are influenced by their wider social interaction and environment (Decety & Somerville, 2003). Individual CEOs, Boards of Directors compromised by 'group think' (Janis 1982) and 'society at large' can endure blind spots that prevent them from seeing (or noticing) painful issues. This stimulates self-deception and cripples timely and effective responses. For instance, market trends turning against organisations create a stress and pain for executives with a strong vested interest in performance. The brain can 'block' or mute these happenings by refusing to see or acknowledge them, so dimming cognition until it is too late. Hence, the 'range of thinking and doing' is limited by what the executives 'fail to notice'. By extension, whole societies can fall asleep, closing minds to the unequal distribution of wealth, environmental degradation, mass migration, mass poverty, undermining of democratic institutions, resource scarcity, slavery and threats of nuclear war.

The progressive enlightening of the strategic management domain by research in social psychology in the 1980s (e.g. Huff, 1982) challenged the then dominant orthodoxy, which was derived from industrial organisation theory. The latter's world view proposed that market structure determined the behaviour of firms and that behaviour determined their performance. Inherently, the contextual environment was 'given' in an objective and exogenous way. The social psychological approach brought the view that these contexts might be endogenously determined, interpreted through the mental models (or 'frames' – see Daft & Weick, 1984) of executives or managers who decode market signals of varying speed and complexity. These 'frames' enabled sophisticated signals to be comprehended by the application of simplifying filters (March & Simon, 1958).

Informed by the lead of Douglas (1986),[50] executives and managers in different organisations in different societies, or even in the same society, will likely perceive their contexts in different ways. They may identify with a specific strategic group (McGee & Thomas, 1986 and/or a certain way of doing things (e.g. as in the notion of industry recipes – see Spender, 1989). The research coupling of cognition and strategy required precise measurement instruments and cognitive accuracy (Milliken, 1990; Sutcliffe, 1994) and progressed to linking cognition to strategy performance (Elsbach et al., 2005) and associated political processes (Kaplan, 2008). How managers perceived became known as 'situated cognition', which Elsbach et al.

---

[50] See chapter 1, p. 3.

(2005) describe as momentary perception in managerial contextual sense making. This early experimental work[51] has been criticised for being methodologically inaccurate, too focussed on US large firms and too case – based to be generalisable. Even so, it established the proposition that managerial cognition, especially perception, is unique and situated in, and maybe influenced by, its own cultural context.

In the IL process, outcome scenarios become the filters that help executives and managers make better sense of plausible, alternative futures and so enable better sense giving within their own organisations (e.g., Gioia & Chittipeddi, 1991). Further, the building of a future scenario coupled with a gripping narrative is a powerful catalyst in unfreezing mental ossification (Boje, 1991; Bowman et al., 2013; Jefferson, 2012) and stimulating the brain's creative elements. Recent research in neuroscience utilising fMRI has helped to make explicit the brain's internal, neural networks that light up when recalling the past and imagining the future (e.g. Schacter & Madore, 2016). The understanding of the process of scenario thinking is in its infancy, but a knowledge base is under construction. For instance, research has shown that the levering of existing knowledge is coupled with areas of the brain that expect reward(s) and knowledge discovery is linked to areas that handle attentional control, and that the levering and pioneering of knowledge uses different neural processing systems (Laureiro-Martinez et al., 2015). We investigate this further in the next section.

6.3 Understanding Memories of the Future

6.3.1 Role of Neuroscience: Episodic Memory

Since the turn of the century, access to functional magnetic resonance imaging (fMRI) technology has brought neuroscience methodology into the path of social scientists e.g. law, political science, anthropology and sociology As Powell (2011) notes, its importation into the management field was a little slower, but penetration soon followed in human resource management, leadership, strategic management and marketing (see Suomala et al., 2012). In particular, marketing has a long history of using psychological approaches to understand consumer behaviour and fMRI-based research took hold quickly in areas like the explanation of consumer preferences (McClure et al., 2004); consumer choice (Lusk et al., 2015) and even chocolate consumption (Kuhn et al., 2016). Expectedly, these approaches have drawn criticism for their actual cost (fMRI time is expensive) and the opportunity

---

[51] For reviews of the field in the early days, see Walsh (1995) and Hodgkinson (1997).

cost through the diversion of scarce research funds (Dovido et al., 2008); ethical challenges (Eser et al., 2011); interpretation and comparability of results (Logothetis, 2008); differences in results (replicability) between healthy and non-healthy subjects (due to brain plasticity); and an over focus on an isolated part of the brain when the brain is a larger, complex muscle that 'thinks, feels, believes and sees' (Bennett & Hacker, 2003). Advances in technology and its gain in legitimacy in the academic literature, however, indicate an endurance in the management domain. Clearly, recalling the past and thinking about multiple future scenarios are cognitive processes that lend themselves readily to investigation by the new technology.

The prospective nature of the brain is a recent feature of psychological research. For decades, research (including both behaviourism and Freudianism) had a 'driven by the past framework' where 'habits and drives were claimed to be universally applicable models of learning, memory, decision-making, motivation and cognition' (Seligman et al., 2013, p. 136). For instance, Bartlett (1932), in his 'theory of remembering', showed how people synthesise past detail in their present social context, so a memory from a story from their poorer schooldays might be enhanced to consider their relatively richer current circumstances e.g. a canoe in early narrative might become a boat, or even a yacht in their present identity. Besides distortions from social conditioning, the brain struggles to assemble materials from the past in a perfect reproductive manner (Anderson & Schooler, 1991). According to Schacter (1999), its recall is troubled by 'commissioned sins' during recall. For instance, the brain stores information about the past in different places to avoid overload. When asked to recall an event, it goes back into its different storage files and brings up what it can in a memory 'mosaic'. Then, it invents any missing material to make a clearer picture which becomes the closest possible replica of the past that it can muster. But graver errors occur when it retrieves material from similar events to the one asked for, and the recalled materials get mixed up in the mosaic and the memory becomes a distorted reflection, rather than a close replica. For decades after Bartlett's theory, memory research was locked into the past, leaving knowledge of the prospective brain and how it linked the past, through the present, to an imagined future as pure conjecture (Suddendorf & Corbalis, 1997; Szpunar et al., 2014).

The seminal work of Kahneman and Tversky (1973) altered this focus by hinting that patterns of similarity might be influential in the brain's recognition. They found that the probability of a future event happening was likely to be higher if the brain had witnessed something like it before, and that if it had not happened before, subjects *invented* future scenarios – with higher probabilities attached to scenarios that were easy to build. Later, focussing on brain simulations in experiments on 'memories of the future', Ingvar (1979, 1985) found heavier blood flows to the prefrontal cortex when at rest, prompting the conclusion that this area is prominent for planning activity: 'The brain ... is automatically busy with extrapolations of future events and, it appears, constructing alternative hypothetical behaviour patterns to be ready for what may happen' (Ingvar, 1979, p. 21).

Sadly, it was not until the advent of fMRI two decades later that Ingvar's pioneering work found any enlightenment in academic research. Analysing neural networks in subjects focussing on past recall and future imagining has advanced memory research, opening new avenues in the past–future brain linkage. Memory is divided into semantic (general knowledge), procedural (skills and routines) and episodic (recollection of past events), and most of this recent research links episodic memory to future imaginings. Suddendorf and Corbalis (1997) show that episodic memory influences people's ability to perform 'mental time travel' – experiencing events in the past and imagining events that might occur in the future. This ability may begin as early as three to five years old (Botzung et al., 2008) and is processed through a common neural network.

Schacter and Madore (2016) placed emphasis on prospection by assuming, like Ingvar, that the brain's core function is to store material to enable it to perceive future contexts. Like Botzung et al. (2008), they assume a neural network common to both recall and future imagining. Their neuroimaging work using fMRI confirms this common network and identifies the subsystems within it that 'light' up more when people think about the past and other subsystems (e.g. the medial frontopolar cortex, the left angular gyrus and the hippocampus) that shine brighter when thinking forward (see also Addis et al., 2009). Because the brain has encoded past materials and stored them, it does not find thinking about the past too difficult. But, the future is unknown, so the brain has no experience or pattern on which to draw. The brighter lights mean it is trying much harder. Hence, subsystems like the hippocampus get 'hot' as the brain is challenged by the uncertain and unseen future domain (Schacter et al., 2013). Further, fMRI has revealed other parts of the core network that are associated directly with specific future prospecting e.g. dorso-medial prefrontal cortex when simulating people; the inferior frontal and premotor cortices when considering objects and locations; and the retrosplenial, parahippocampal and parietal cortices when thinking about locations (Hassabis et al., 2013; Szpunar & Schacter, 2013). These elements of the core network produce correlated activity. In further research, Thakral, Madore and Schacter (2017) have begun to break down the individual components and see what effect they have on episodic memory and episodic simulation. They show how disruption of the left angular gyrus (lag) leads to significant reductions in internal (who, what, where) episodic detail and an increase in external (semantic) detail, and conclude how significant the lag is for both memory and forward simulation.

The same network seems to operate for counterfactual thinking as well, though Schacter et al. warn that:

> Though episodic future thinking and episodic counter factual thinking require similar constructive processes, these operate on material that is differentially constrained by reality. The future is inherently uncertain, and thus there are many degrees of freedom in simulating prospective episodes, and any mental mutation of the past may clash with our knowledge of the events wider context.
>
> (Schacter et al., 2013, p. 17)

Other cognitive research has shown that as people imagine a future scenario repeatedly, their belief in its happening increases greatly (Carroll, 1978) and this applies to the people, objects and locations within it (Szpunar & Schacter, 2013). For the IL process in scenario planning, repeated simulations would allow people to 'pre-feel' their position in an imagined scenario and maybe accept its plausibility the more they think it through. Hence, this 'lived future experience' that taps into emotions about a future with potential behavioural responses in the present has been linked to long-term strategy and decision-making (Gilbert & Wilson, 2007).

6.3.2 Role of Neuroscience: Non-Episodic Memory

Elements of semantic memory, working alongside episodic memory, play a significant role in connecting the past to the future. Irish et al. (2012) and Klein (2013) claim that semantic memory influences perceptions of the past and prospecting for the future. Younger adults tend to be better at recalling the specifics (who, when, where issues) of past events than older adults, while the latter are better at the infusion of more general external information like comparisons between facts in different recalled events (e.g. different weddings over time), reflections and the relative importance of issues (Addis et al., 2008). Rendell et al. (2012) claim that this is due to changes in episodic memory systems though, Schacter and Madore (2016) found that even under conditions when the episodic memory is not taxed, older adults have less precise description and more comparisons in their recollections than younger adults.

Scientists have tried to tease out the impact of episodic and non-episodic memory on recalling the past and imagining the future by rehearsing past events with subjects (Madore et al., 2014). Using the Cognitive Interview[52] (Fisher & Geiselman, 1992) to induct participants into a recall of the past event, they found an increase in internal detail recall in episodic memory for *all* adults but, no effect on the volume of external details in semantic memory for either age group. Importantly for the IL scenario process: 'Age related changes in remembering the past and imagining the future reflect primarily the operation of non-episodic mechanisms, such as changes in narrative style or communicative goals that occur with ageing and could affect performance similarly on memory, imagination, and picture description tasks' (Schacter & Madore, 2016, p. 6).

Rehearsing the construction of scenes of places, objects and people in this way might help participants to adapt more easily to similar scenes should they occur e.g. organisations (especially the emergency services) often rehearse 'crisis' scenarios (Hassabis & Maguire, 2007). Contextually, it seems that when thinking about future 'scenes' that have a lot of reflection in past experiences, episodic memory is dominant, but when thinking about unfamiliar things in the future (e.g. especially those that, in Kahn's words, mean 'thinking the unthinkable'), semantic memory is dominant (Anderson, 2012; Klein et al., 2012). Hence, the best approach to making 'memories of the future' might be for future scenes to be created through semantic memory but built upon the brain's collection of pre-existing episodic memories (McLelland et al., 2015). McKiernan notes that:

> However, such studies rely on participant's scene familiarity and so on future scene construction that is similar to past scenes. Importantly, scene construction involves imagining scenes that do not rely on episodic memory alone but are more generic in their settings – like scenarios of the future. Human and organisational adaptation requires the mental capability to imagine future scenes that are unfamiliar but could happen. It may be the case that general settings draw upon some part of individual episodic memory, but the extent is not yet known.
>
> (McKiernan, 2017)

Investigating the recall within and across three societal sets (Hiking Club, Friends, Family), van Mulukom et al. (2016) provide some answers. They found that scenes created within sets were rated as more plausible and recalled more often than those across the sets (the ones containing more uncertainty in

---

[52] A technique used to increase event recall in eyewitnesses that is designed to maximise the accuracy of memory retrieval and minimise misinformation and false memories. Memory fades with time, and so it is important to encode information as soon as feasible and ensure that the conditions at encoding are as close as possible to the conditions at the time of retrieval (from McKiernan, 2017).

the form of unfamiliarity). For scenario planners, it is noteworthy that cross-set scenes were deemed to happen in longer futures and needed much more brain effort than within-set ones. Recall of scenes was mainly due to memories that the brain had codified already.

These scenes are closely analogous to the creation of scenarios about multiple future states. Scenario building in the IL process involves thinking imaginatively about different future settings and then thinking logically through the cause–effect trajectory that links the present to these deep future scenarios. Powell (2011) points out that the aggregation of groups (e.g. firms) as units of analysis in strategic management means that there is a limited scope for a brain-scanning technique like fMRI, that rely on data collected at an individual level. But participants in an IL process work at both the individual and group levels, thus opening up a more generous scope for brain imaging in the foresight process to understand scenario thinking better.

Many of these cognitive science findings impact the scenario-building stage of the IL process (see Figure 1). The prior stages (data collection to key issue identification) can be underpinned by good methodological science, but the building stage is largely a human endeavour. Fortification by research in cognitive and neuroscience might 'lift' the technical construction and the human imagination in scenario building, enhancing scenario vividness and protecting scenario planning from accusations of a cognitive 'failure of imagination' (Patel, 2016). The application of science to scenario thinking within scenario planning has much in common with the research agendas in cognitive neuroscience that explore recall in the past and imaginings of future states. Much can be learned from the infusion of one with the other though, as Gilbert and Wilson (2007) point out, awareness of the brain's limitations is essential. In particular, errors in its prospecting systems can limit the accuracy of future scene building. This can occur through inaccurate recall of memories of the past, an over focus on the central and not the peripheral themes in a future scene, an emphasis on synthesis rather than detail in future scenes and a precedence given to today's contextual forces rather than those bearing upon a future state. They note that: 'The cortex attempts to trick the rest of the brain by impersonating a sensory system. It simulates future events to find out what the subcortical structures know, but try as it might, the cortex cannot generate simulations that have all the richness and reality of genuine perceptions' (Gilbert & Wilson, 2007, p. 1354).

Scenario thinkers need to be alert to the brain's trickery in scenario thinking and guard against it privileging the familiar over the unknown, the memorable over the unimaginable, the generic over the specific, the early years over the later ones in a scenario and current drivers of change over those acting on the future horizon. Despite these limitations, there is evidence to suggest that such thinking enhances managerial judgement. We turn our attention to this in the next section.

7 Scenario Thinking and Managerial Judgement

Chance is commonly viewed as a self-correcting process in which a deviation in one direction induces a deviation in the opposite direction to restore the equilibrium. In fact, deviations are not 'corrected' as a chance process unfolds, they are merely diluted.

A. Tversky and D. Kahneman (1974, p. 1125)

Proponents of scenario planning as a tool for improving managerial judgement frequently point out that its primary benefit is in influencing the mindsets of senior managers. In his seminal articles on scenario planning, Wack (1985a, 1985b) argued that scenarios are aimed at the microcosms – inner mental models – that senior managers construct about the world around them. Referring to the behavioural foundations of scenario planning, Schoemaker remarks that: 'In my view, they represent a fundamentally different approach to dealing with uncertainty and complexity, in that the method is focused on characteristic biases of the human mind such as over confidence and anchoring' (Schoemaker, 1993, p. 196). In addition, van der Heijden (1996) points to the schemas of the world that managers bring to bear when thinking about the future, and the role that scenarios have in interrogating such schemas. Yet these many claims for the cognitive benefit of scenario thinking lack rigorous testing (Harries, 2003), and remain largely 'anecdotal' (Schoemaker, 2004, p. 288).

While limited, the empirical evidence on the cognitive benefit of scenario thinking for managerial judgement has produced mixed results. These have led some scholars to argue whether scenarios reduce overconfidence. In laboratory studies using student participants, Schoemaker (1993) found that they did, implying that scenarios are a useful cognitive aid, whilst Kuhn and Sniezek (1996) found they did not. Tetlock (2005), in a series of experiments investigating the impact of scenarios on expert judgement, found that they have a propensity to increase confusion for those who are cognitively inclined to be open-minded, while they fail to open the minds of those cognitively disinclined to be open-minded. By contrast, Meissner and Wulf (2013) found in their laboratory studies that scenario planning reduces the framing bias.

Some scholars have argued that practitioner self-reported successes of scenario methods, particularly as they pertain to the most commonly applied intuitive logics method and its derivatives, lack reliable results as to what worked and what did not (Wilkinson, 2009). Other field studies have had varying results. Hodgkinson and Wright (2002) reported on a failed scenario-planning intervention, which they analysed using Janis and Mann's (1979) conflict theory of decision-making. They attributed the failure of scenarios to have an impact on the managerial judgement of a cognitively disparate senior management team to defensive avoidance strategies and psychodynamics of the CEO and the team, caused by the decisional stress of having to confront a range of alternatives.

Criticisms of the design of their intervention (Whittington, 2006) led indirectly to further work outlining a number of design propositions that incorporate personality, social categorisation and social identity parameters into the scenario process. These indicate the importance of the social, as well as the psychological, dimensions of this process (Hodgkinson & Healey, 2008). For example, Phadnis et al. (2015) conducted a number of experiments with experts in the freight business to assess whether pre-constructed scenarios had any effects on long-term investment decisions. They found that the use of multiple scenarios had little impact on the confidence of expert judgements on investment evaluations, but they did indicate a preference for options and solutions that have higher flexibility to implement their investment decisions. Poignantly, this study suggests that such 'de-biasing' cognitive benefits derived from scenario planning arise when the entire process is followed, which is in stark contrast to other laboratory studies that use simple, pre-constructed, stimulation-response scenarios to assess cognitive impact.

In the experiments reported on by Tetlock (2005), for instance, the participants used in the studies were a combination of experts and dilettantes who were put through successive rounds of assessments that required them to make probability judgements on sets of pre-constructed scenarios. This implies that it is the *process* of constructing scenarios, rather than the scenarios themselves, that aid cognition when thinking about the future. Likewise, Phadnis et al. (2015) acknowledge that their controlled experiments in the field do not reflect the way that organisations use scenarios, particularly for those that use them continuously.

Thus, controlled experiments on the influence of pre-conceived and constructed scenarios may be misleading. Scenario practitioners have long emphasised the importance of the process by which scenarios are constructed and its role in 'disciplining' imagination (Schoemaker, 1997), especially in the consequent strategic conversations that permeate organisational board rooms (cf. van der Heijden, 1996). In experiments on whether scenario thinking can reduce overconfidence, Schoemaker (1995) found that there was little evidence that being involved in the process itself versus considering scenarios that others have developed has any bearing in reducing overconfidence. However, he points out that taking intellectual ownership of scenarios by being involved in the process increases their credibility and thus, it can be inferred, of the judgements that are influenced by them.

A further body of evidence suggests that many of the biases associated with strategic decision-making can be mitigated through relatively simple pencil-and-paper methods (e.g. Arkes et al., 1981; Koriat et al., 1980; Wright & Goodwin, 2002). For example, studies in medicine that test diagnostics suggest that listing and, critically, elaborating on the rational for choosing between alternatives, can reduce overconfidence in outcomes and enhance learning (Arkes et al., 1988; Koriat et al., 1980). Thinking about alternatives thus appears to prime the pump for judgement, decision-making and behaviour (Galinsky & Moskowitz, 2000), particularly when the process involves cutting through large numbers of possibilities and distilling them down into a small number of possible alternatives that reflect a range of uncertainties (cf. Schoemaker, 1995). Yet, while evidence suggests that de-biasing decision-making and judgement is possible, it implies also that individuals are often not capable of de-biasing themselves (Hogarth, 2001; Kahneman, 2003; Sanna & Schwarz, 2003), necessitating interventions (Larrick, 2004) like scenario thinking.

Indeed, Kahneman (2003) has popularised the notion of the system one and the system two modes of thinking. System one modes of thinking are largely automatic, intuitive and fast moving, and allow individuals to navigate the world in a generally effortless and unconscious way. By contrast, system two is more controlled, deliberative, effortful and slow. Both systems operate simultaneously, but system two is normally mobilised when in a relatively routinised, rules-based, procedural culture one encounters a discrepancy or surprise that requires a conscious effort to address. Most of the time, it is system one that shapes thoughts, weaves contextual stories and informs judgement. Because system one is largely automatic and unconscious, it can be prone to a range of distorting cognitive biases; but, as Kahneman et al. (2011) argue, moving from the individual strategic decision-maker to the collective process of the organisation through scenario thinking is an approach that can help to mitigate such biases. Scenarios in themselves are unlikely to be enough; the process by which stories are constructed is an essential cognitive aid to improving strategic decision-making.

However, as with the individual, scholars have emphasised that the capabilities, processes, relationships and structures comprising social systems, such as organisations, have a bearing on behaviour by where they distribute the attention of decision-makers (Ocasio, 1997). Levinthal and Rerup (2006, p. 504) argue that organisational attentional engagement, such as through information processing, can be distinguished between automatic (or less mindful), and controlled (or more mindful). They postulate that the ability to respond to signals, or unanticipated cues, is closely associated with attentiveness or mindfulness of context. While organisational attention involves complex mechanisms and trade-offs (Ocasio, 2011), well-designed scenario processes are a useful aid for enhancing forward-looking attentional perspectives. Research suggests that these help organisations to overcome inertial propensities and enhance managerial discretion in their environments (cf. Ocasio, 2011, p. 1293; also see Hambrick & Finkelstein, 1995).

Scenario thinking, while possessing the intuitive qualities of system one, also relates closely to system two – conscious, deliberative, effortful, modes of thinking. This aids managerial judgement by improving the quality of strategic decision-making, but necessitates the overcoming of individual cognitive biases that creep into the system one mode of thinking. Moreover, as individual thinking is freed up, organisational inertia, often embedded in the dominant logics (Bettis & Prahalad, 1995) that guides organisational behaviour as a whole, is loosened. Scenario thinking has important implications for system one thinking. As an automatic mode of thinking that relies heavily on what Ingvar (1985) called 'memories of the future' (the schemas of action that, based on past experiences, become stored in memory), scenario thinking may bolster system one thinking by expanding experiences in an imaginative way. In other words, as with grandmasters of chess (e.g. Kasparov, 2005), being able to identify patterns quickly, exercise good judgement with a multiplicity of possible moves and under time pressure, and to adapt to changing circumstances in the environment quickly, scenario thinking helps to broaden the requisite variety of memories, and thus patterns, that strategic decision makers draw on, automatically and intuitively.

8 Conclusion

Not wholly consciously, but not quite unconsciously, as far as I can remember, I determined to fashion my future as a sculptor his marble, and there was in it the same mixture of foresight and the unknown. The thing in the mind of the artist takes its way and imposes its form as it wakens under his hand. And so with life.

F. Stark, British-Italian explorer and writer

Of a great metaphysician/ he looked at (into?) his own Soul with a Telescope/ what seemed all irregular, he saw and shewed to be beautiful Constellations and he added to the Consciousness hidden worlds within worlds.

Samuel Taylor Coleridge, Notebooks (CN I 1798)

In our brief Element, the deep history of future prospecting from the ancient Babylonians, through military war gaming, to the dominant French and Anglo-American schools of today is illustrated. During this journey, we uncovered the unreferenced British prospecting experience. From the broad portfolio of existing scenario-planning processes developed through time, the focus was on the intuitive logics version, as attention turned to thinking rather than planning. Through a stage-based approach, it was shown how IL maximises people's involvement, and relies heavily on their powers of both logical thinking and creative imagination. There followed an exploration of the cognitive challenge of managerial judgement and how an individual's immersion in the scenario process appears more beneficial than the alternative scenario stories that emerge from it. Then, we linked existing cognitive analyses to the relatively new findings in neuroscience, to isolate key research findings with a hope of improving our intuitive logics, those of other scenario facilitators and those of executives and managers who utilise the process.

But we acknowledge that embedding scenario thinking in well-established organisations is not easy. Existing belief systems, path-dependent planning processes, age-old perspectives, emergencies and past successes can act to reject proactive thinking. Often, the stronger the sentiment expressed about 'the way things are done around here' is often a warning of the extent of mental calcification in an organisation and an indication of the difficulties that are likely to be faced in affecting serious strategic change. Yet the weight of psychological evidence, and the endurance of scenario planning over the past five decades in all types of organisations, suggests that the process of thinking about the future terrain, and the imagining of alternative futures related to it, can have a powerful influence on the creative aspects of human behaviour, as well as polish decision-making in the present. In addition, we acknowledge that much further research is required.

8.1 Further Research

The shift from viewing scenario planning as a tool to seeing scenario thinking as a heuristic with its concomitant cognitive implications presents a number of investigative opportunities for scholars to explore, especially through cooperation with neuroscientists. First, personal imaginings with much self-referencing have been found to be different from general, future imaginings (Courtney et al., 1997; Pighin et al., 2011). This raises the question of how the extent of personal involvement in the future to be imagined (e.g. by a CEO with KPI targets or a small firm owner-manager) varies with the nature of the scenario set constructed. Moreover, how does personal interest influence the scenario-building process (e.g. by a dominant personality bias)?

Second, the ageing process has been shown to influence the type of recall detail with older adults using more semantic external knowledge and less episodic internal knowledge than younger adults (Schacter et al., 2015). Do younger adults create more detailed and less generic scenarios than older adults?

Third, memory-enhancing techniques like the Cognitive Interview have been shown to improve the detail in recall and in future imagining by up to 12 per cent in eyewitness research (Geiselman et al., 1985). Does the prior use of memory-enhancing techniques[53] improve recall of past events/trends across age groups? Can prior rehearsal of thinking about future imaginings lead to richer scenarios than no rehearsal?

Fourth, subjects can recall scenes more easily that are constructed with familiar information, events and people. Moreover, subjects rate plausibility more highly with such familiarity (van Mulukon et al., 2016). Rehearsal techniques improve this detail of this recall (see earlier in this volume). But scenario building requires imagining of the unknown, which the brain struggles to encode as future memory (Ingvar, 1985). Are specific scenario scenes close to the scenario builder (e.g. in their organisational sector) easier to build and rated as more plausible than generic ones? Are scenarios with familiar components accepted too readily at the scenario testing stage?

Fifth, perceptions of scenarios viewed as 'good' or 'bad' can induce physical responses in subjects when they could envisage themselves in the scene: 'Guided by the assumption that imagined scenarios retain essential properties (e.g., spatial, temporal, perceptual, motoric) of the events they represent, neuroimaging and behavioral research has revealed considerable overlap in the operations (i.e., neural, cognitive) that support both mental simulation and actual behaviour' (Miles et al., 2014, p. 558). Do scenarios contain more positive elements than negative ones? Are plausibility rankings higher for scenarios packed with positive features than those that are not?

Sixth, criticism has filtered into the literature about whether scenario thinking leads to a re-evaluation of assumptions and fresh perceptions, or creates confusion or reinforces existing views (e.g. Phadnis et al., 2015;

---

[53] Scientists have warned of the consequences of over rehearsal that lead subjects to give higher plausibility to constantly reimagined scenes (Szpunar & Schacter, 2013).

Tetlock, 2005). Yet, these results have been derived from relatively controlled studies, rather than the messiness of strategic decision-making in organisational contexts. Such studies also privilege cold cognition over affective/ emotional and nonconscious cognitive processes (e.g. Hodgkinson & Healey, 2011). Revisiting such findings in natural settings has the potential to yield much deeper insights into scenario thinking, and to lead to improved processes.

Finally, scholars posit that organisational behaviour results from how the attention of decision-makers is channelled and distributed within firms based on the relationships, resources and rules that constitute them (Ocasio, 1997, 2011). Clearly there is a cognitive dimension to this process, and how scenarios are distributed within firms, and which ones receive the attention of decision-makers has implications for explaining organisational adaptation and behaviour.

As these questions, and others, are answered, our knowledge of scenario thinking and the design of an optimal scenario process will deepen. The research is ceaseless.

8.2 Concluding Caveat

In the scenario-thinking process, the conscious mind finds a friend in the unconscious psyche. In union, they discover a fresh vision of how worlds might be. Coleridge, whose quotation greets this section, saw the alchemy in this union as making his theory of poetry a 'rationalised dream' – a term closely related to the nomenclature of 'intuitive logics'. A hundred years later, Carl Jung – who inspired the field of analytical psychology – explained dreaming in much the same manner:

> What is repressed, ignored or neglected by the conscious is compensated by the unconscious . . . and the dream gives clues that, if properly read, to those functions and archetypes of the psyche pressing, at the moment, for recognition.
>
> Carl Gutsav Jung (1968, p. 13)

The demands of making strategy in modern organisations compete with the time and seclusion needed to tap into the unconscious mind and to couple it to conscious thought and to see the 'beautiful constellations' ahead. But without such imagination, executive teams can be blind to fruitful pathways over the terrain and, end up in much the same place as they began. Scenario thinking might be the alchemists' 'gold'.

Step	Description	Indicative literature
One	Defining the focal issue, key stakeholders and horizon year (how far into the future the scenarios will look)	e.g. Burt & van der Heijden, 2003; Cairns et al., 2016
Two	Generating a list of 'forces' or 'trends' driving the future, normally using a PESTEL (political, economic, social, technological, environmental and legal) framework initially through a combination of brainstorming and research	e.g. Burt et al., 2006; Wright & Goodwin, 2009; Wright et al., 2013
Three	Clustering the driving forces using causal mapping or influence diagrams	e.g. Wright & Goodwin, 2009
Four	Ranking these clustered forces based on their importance/impact on shaping the future environment	e.g. van der Heijden, et al., 2002; Wright & Cairns, 2011.
Five	Identifying the 'predetermined' or 'forecastable' forces from those that are uncertain	e.g. Wack, 1985a, 1985b
Six	Using no fewer than two, and no more than four of the most highly ranked uncertainties, exploring how 'predetermined' forces might interact with key 'uncertainties' in a causal chain that establishes a 'roll-out' of the logics and a skeletal storyline. This can be done 'deductively', using a 2 X 2 matrix, or 'inductively', letting the roll-out evolve organically.	e.g. van der Heijden, et al., 2002; Ramirez et al., 2013; van Klooster & Asselt, 2006; Schoemaker, 1991; Wack, 1985a, 1985b
Seven	Fleshing out the storylines by developing the interactions and events that lead to the scenario	e.g. Bowman et al., 2013; Schwartz, 1991
Eight	Testing the scenarios for internal coherence, plausibility, surprise and gestalt (how the scenario fits together to reflect the range of uncertainties identified	e.g. van der Heijden et al, 2002; Wack, 1985a, 1985b; Wright & Cairns, 2011

(cont.)

Step	Description	Indicative literature
Nine	Identifying 'sign-posts' and 'early warning systems' (key events that can be used to monitor whether a scenario or element of a scenario is coming to pass	e.g. Derbyshire & Wright, 2014; Ramirez et al., 2013; Tucker, 2007
Ten	Considering the implications of the scenarios for strategy and/or strategic decisions	e.g. Goodwin & Wright, 2001; Schoemaker & van der Heijden, 1992; O'Brien et al., 2007; O'Brien & Meadows, 2013; Wilson, 2000; Wright & Goodwin, 2009

Source: MacKay and Stoyanova (2017)

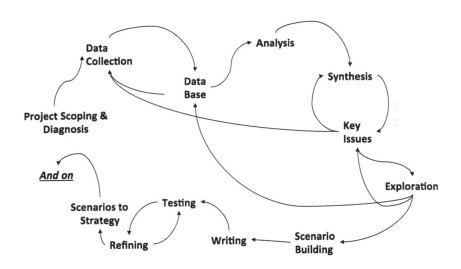

Figure 1 Diagrammatic representation of a generic 'intuitive logics' process

(Developed from McKiernan, 2017)

Appendix
Probabilistic Modified Trends

Trend Impact Analysis (TIA)

TIA has a logical two-part method. First, time series data are collected on key variables and the projection calculated as if in a traditional forecast and a 'surprise-free' future is estimated. Recognising that the past is only partly perfect in predicting the future, a second stage of judgement and imagination is employed. Here, expert opinion attaches probabilities to future events that might impact the original projection. The events should be both plausible and highly impactful, and verifiable *ex poste*. The expected value is achieved by summation and multiplication of these probabilities and impacts, given their time lags. The software produces a new 'fit' with a range constrained by upper and lower boundary limits. Besides combining forecasting with human judgement and avoiding a single-point estimate, TIA helps quantify a scenario set, so increasing the perception of a 'science' and arguably, of the internal consistency of the set (a key test in the IL process). Gordon and Glenn (1994) claim that the TIA method is used frequently, but others challenge this assertion within the scenario literature (Bradfield et al., 2005).

Cross-Impact Analysis (CIA)

CIA[1] has the same heritage of source (RAND), purpose and construction (incorporation of probabilities) as TIA, but it differs in adding conditional probabilities. Gordon and Glenn explain that CIA came about through asking 'can forecasting be based on perceptions about how future events may interact?' (1994; p. 1) The initial exploration was through a card game (Future) developed for the Kaiser that contained events determined by probabilities (as in TIA) using a custom die and a history of how these events had occurred in the past. The key contribution and departure from TIA is the assumption that events are determined by other events and by the prevailing context, both of which influence the probability of an event occurring. Hence, the technique connects events (E) to key drivers (D) of change (variables) and allocates either a positive or negative impact from E to D and so 'most likely' and 'least likely' scenarios can be developed. As in TIA, expert analysts are at the heart of the

---

[1] Note that there are two strands to the CIA, one developed by futurists and the other by intelligence agencies. The approaches are similar, but the methods are slightly different.

process through the allocation of the nature and number of events chosen; the *a priori* event probabilities individually; the conditional probabilities of each event's impact on another in the event set (If A happens, what is the likelihood of B happening and so on); the interpretation of simulation tests; and the production of the final scenario sets (Gordon & Glenn, 1994).

Over the years, many computer simulation models have been developed around the CIA, including BASICS (Battelle) and INTERAX (University of California). Indeed, the cross-fertilisation between the French school and the American school continued as Godet (with Duperrin) developed their own cross-impact software (SMIC) for prospecting in France (Gordon & Glenn, 1994). Unlike IL, and despite the extent of the mathematical modelling involved, the variation in approach and software is minimal while the link to TIA through human expert judgement via the use of another RAND product (Delphi) remains very strong.

Table 2 Comparison of the similarities and differences between the American and French schools of thought

Scenario Process	Intuitive Logics	*La Prospective*	Probabalistic Modified Trends
Similarities			
Scenario horizon	3–20 years plus	3–20 years	3–20 years
Scenario initiation	Specific problem/issue	Specific problem/issue	Specific problem/issue related to time series data
Differences			
Project purpose	Multiple – learning, strategy, anticipating, sense-making	One-off – strategy/ policy	One-off – policy
Scenario perspective	Descriptive/ normative	Descriptive/ normative	Descriptive
Scope	Broad or narrow	Narrow	Narrow
Method focus	Process	Outcome	Outcome
	Inductive/ deductive	Directed & objective	Directed & objective

Table 2 (cont.)

Scenario Process	Intuitive Logics	*La Prospective*	Probabalistic Modified Trends
	Subjective Qualitative	Quantitative & computers	Quantitative & computers
Scenario team	Internal	Internal/external expert	External experts
Role of scenario expert	Project facilitator	Project leader	Project leader
Tools	Generic	Proprietary	Proprietary
	Ideas generation	MICMAC software	Trend-impact analysis
	PESTLE analysis	MACTOR software	Cross-impact analysis
	Clustering	Morphological Analysis	Monte Carlo simulation
	Soft systems	Delphi	MACTOR software
	Stakeholder analysis	SMIC software	
	Delphi	MULTIPOL software	
	Matrices	Delphi	
Selection of key drivers	Intuition	Interviews	Time series data trends
	Ideas generation	Structural analysis	Expert judgement
	Interviews		
	Remarkable people		
Scenario set construction	Matrices	Matrices	Monte Carlo simulations
Project Output	Qualitative	Qualitative & Quantitative	Quantitative
	Narrative	Detailed analysis	Short story lines
	Graphs	Actions and consequences	
	Pictures		
	Poetry		
	Montage		
Probabilities	No	Yes	Yes, conditional
Scenario number	2–4	Multiple	3–6

Table 2 (cont.)

Scenario Process	Intuitive Logics	*La Prospective*	Probabalistic Modified Trends
Scenario tests	Internal consistency	Internal consistency	Plausible
	Gestalt	Gestalt	Verifiable
	Surprise	Plausibility	
	Plausibility	Coherence	
	Coherence	Verifiable ex poste	
Treatment of uncertainty	Inherent and embraced across scenarios	Inherent	Integrated in a stochastic term

Source: Adapted by the authors from Bradfield et al., 2005, with additions from their own practical experience

Bibliography

Abrahamson, E. 1991. Managerial fads and fashions. *Academy of Management Review*, 16, 586–612.

Abrams, M. 1966. *Personal Papers*. Cambridge: Churchill College Cambridge.

Ackoff, R. 1983. Beyond prediction and preparation. *Journal of Management Studies*, 20, 1, 59–69.

Addis, D. R., Pan, L., Vu, M. A., Laiser, N. & Schacter, D. 2009. Constructive episodic simulation of the future and the past: Distinct subsystems of a core brain network mediate imagining and remembering. *Neuropsychologia*, 47, 2222–2238.

Addis, D. R., Wong, A. T. & Schacter, D. L. 2008. Age-related changes in the episodic simulation of future events. *Psychological Science*, 19, 33–41.

Allen, T. B. 1987. *War Games: Inside the Secret World of the Men Who Play at World War III*. London: Heinemann.

Amabile, R. 1995. Scenario planning. *Sloan Management Review*, 36, 7–7.

Amer, M., Daim, T. U. & Jetter, A. 2013. A review of scenario planning. *Futures*, 46, 23–40.

Anderson, R. J. 2012. Imagining novel futures: The roles of event plausibility and familiarity. *Memory*, 20, 443–451.

Anderson, R. J. & Schooler, L. J. 2012. Reflections of the environment in memory. *Psychological Science*, 2, 396–408.

Anikeeva, E., Plotnikov, G., Andguladze, O. & Halivopulo, I. 2016. Developing critical thinking skills in continuing nursing education through visual simulation scenarios. *European Journal of Cardiovascular Nursing*, 15, S81–S81.

Ansoff, H. I. 1975. Managing strategic surprise by response to weak signals. *California Management Review*, 18, 21–33.

Argenti, J. 1968. *Corporate Planning: A Practical Guide*. London: Allen & Unwin.

Argenti, J. 1974. *Systematic Corporate Planning*. London: Nelson.

Arkes, H., Wortmann, R., Saville, P. D. & Harkness, A. 1981. The hindsight bias among physicians weighing the likelihood of diagnoses. *Journal of Applied Psychology*, 66, 252–254.

Ashby, W. R. 1956. *An Introduction to Cybernetics*. London: Chapman & Hall.

Ashby, W. R. 1958. Requisite variety and its implications for the control of complex systems. *Cybernetica (Namur)*, 1, 2, 83–99.

Atherton, A. 2005. A future for small business? Prospective scenarios for the development of the economy based on current policy thinking and counterfactual reasoning. *Futures*, 37, 777–794.

Ayres, R. 2000. On forecasting discontinuities. *Technological Forecasting and Social Change*, 65, 81–97.

Bain, D. & Roubelat, F. 1994. Profutures: The birth of the Strategic Prospective and Futures Studies International Network for Applied Methodology. *Futures*, 26, 345–349.

Barr, P. S., Stimpert, J. L. & Huff, A. S. 1992. Cognitive change, strategic action, and organizational renewal. *Strategic Management Journal*, 13, 15–36.

Bartlett, F. C. 1932. *Remembering: A Study in Experimental and Social Psychology*. Cambridge: Cambridge University Press.

Baskin-Sommers, A. R., Curtin, J. J., Larson, C. L., Stout, D., Kiehl, K. A. & Newman, J. P. 2012. Characterising the anomalous cognition–emotion interactions in externalizing. *Biological Psychology*, 91, 48–58.

Bazerman, M. H. & Watkins, M. 2004. *Predictable Surprises: The Disasters You Should Have Seen Coming, and How to Prevent Them*. Boston, MA: Harvard Business School.

Behrens, T. E., Woolrich, M. W, Walton, M. E. & Rushworth, M. F. 2007. Learning the value of information in an uncertain world. *Nature Neuroscience*, 10, 1214–1221.

Bell, D. G. & Graubard, S. R. (eds.) 1967. *Towards the Year 2000: Work in Progress*. Cambridge, MA: MIT Press.

Bennett, M. R. & Hacker, P. M. S. 2003. *Philosophical Foundations of Neuroscience*. Malden, MA: Blackwell Publishing.

Berger, G. 1964. *Phenomenologie du temps et prospective*. Paris: Presses Universitaires de France.

Bernarde, M. A. 1973. *Our Precarious Habitat*. New York, NY: W. W. Norton & Company.

Bettis, R. & Prahalad, C.-K. 1995. The dominant logic: Retrospective and extension. *Strategic Management Journal*, 16, 5–14.

Bezold, C. 1996. On futures thinking: Trends, scenarios, visions, and strategies. *Quality Progress*, 29, 81–83.

Boje, D. M. 1991. Consulting and change in the storytelling organisation. *Journal of Organisational Change Management*, 4, 7–17.

Boot, M. 2006. *War Made New: Technology, Warfare, and the Course of History, 1500 to Today*. London: Gotham Books.

Botzung, A., Denkova, E. & Manning, L. 2008. Experiencing past and future personal events: Functional neuroimaging evidence on the neural bases of mental time travel. *Brain and Cognition*, 66, 202–212.

Bowman, G., MacKay, R., Masrani, S. & McKiernan, P. 2013. Storytelling and the scenario process: Understanding success and failure. *Technological Forecasting and Social Change*, 80, 735–748.

Bradfield, R., Derbyshire, J. & Wright, G. 2016. The critical role of history in scenario thinking: Augmenting causal analysis within the intuitive logics scenario development methodology. *Futures*, 77, 56–66.

Bradfield, R., Wright, G., Burt, G., Cairns, G. & van der Heijden, K. 2005. The origins and evolution of scenario techniques in long range business planning. *Futures*, 37, 795–812.

Brews, P. J. H. & Hunt, M. R. 1999. Learning to plan and planning to learn: Resolving the planning/learning school debate. *Strategic Management Journal*, 20, 889–913.

Broadbent, D. E. 1958. *Perception and Communication*. London: Pergamon Press.

Broadbent, D. E. & Broadbent, M. H. P. 1987. From detection to identification: Response to multiple targets in rapid serial visual presentation. *Perception & Psychophysics*, 42, 105–113.

Brown, S. 1968. Scenarios in systems analysis. In Quade, E. S. & Boucher, W. I. (eds.) *Systems Analysis and Policy Planning: Applications in Defence*. New York, NY: American Elsevier Publishing Company.

Builder, C. 1996. *50th Project Air Force: 1946–1996*. Washington, DC: RAND Corporation.

Burt, G. & van der Heijden, K. 2003. First steps: Towards purposeful activities in scenario thinking and future studies. *Futures*, 35, 1011–1026.

Buur, J. L., Schmidt, P., Smylie, D., Irizarry, K., Crocker, C., Tyler, J. & Barr, M. 2012. Validation of a scenario-based assessment of critical thinking using an externally validated tool. *Journal of Veterinary Medical Education*, 39, 276–282.

Caffrey, M. 2000. History of war games: Towards a history-based doctrine for wargaming. *Aerospace Power Journal*, Fall, 33–56.

Cairns, G., Wright, G. & Fairbrother, P. 2016. Promoting articulated action from diverse stakeholders in response to public policy scenarios: A case study of the use of 'scenario improvisation' method. *Technological Forecasting and Social Change*, 103, 97–108.

Cairns, G., Wright, G., van der Heijden, K., Bradfield, R. & Burt, G. 2006. Enhancing foresight between multiple agencies: Issues in the use of scenario thinking to overcome fragmentation. *Futures*, 38, 1010–1025.

Carroll, J. S. 1978. The effect of imagining an event on expectations for the event: An interpretation in terms of the availability heuristic. *Journal of Experimental Social Psychology*, 14, 88–96.

Cazes, B. 2008. *Histoire des futurs: les figures de l'avenir de saint Augustin au XXIe siècle*. Paris: L'Harmattan.

Checkland, P. 1981. *Systems Thinking, Systems Practice*. Chichester: Wiley.

Chermack, T. J. 2011. *Scenario Planning in Organizations: How to Create, Use, and Assess Scenarios*. San Francisco, CA: Berrett-Koehler.

Chiang, Y. 1936. *The Chinese Eye*. London: Methuen & Company Ltd.

Clegg, S. & Bailey, J. R. (eds.) 2008. *International Encyclopedia of Organization Studies*, Vol. 1. London: Sage.

Courtney, H., Kirkland, J. & Viguerie, P. 1997. Strategy under uncertainty. *Harvard Business Review*, 75, 66–79.

Cummings, S. & Daellenbach, U. 2009. A guide to the future of strategy? The history of long range planning. *Long Range Planning*, 42, 234–263.

Curnow, T. 2004. *The Oracles of the Ancient World: A Complete Guide*. London: Duckworth.

Daft, R. L. & Weick, K. E. 1984. Toward a model of organizations as interpretation systems. *Academy of Management Review*, 9, 284–295.

de Jouvenal, B. 1964. *L'Art de la conjecture*. Monaco.

de Jouvenal, B. 1967. *The Art of Conjecture*. New York, NY: Basic Books.

de Jouvenal, B. 1972. *Du Principat: et autres reflexions politiques* [S.l.]. Hachette.

de Molina, L. 1988. *On Divine Foreknowledge (Part IV of the Concordia)*. Ithaca, NY: Cornell University Press.

Decety, J. & Sommerville, J. A. 2003. Shared representations between self and other: A social cognitive neuroscience view. *TRENDS in Cognitive Science*, 7, 527–533.

Derbyshire, J. & Wright, G. 2014. Preparing for the future: Development of an 'antifragile' methodology that compliments scenario planning by omitting causation. *Technological Forecasting and Social Change*, 82, 215–225.

Douglas, M. 1986. *How Institutions Think*. London: Routledge & Kegan Paul.

Douglas, M. & Wildavsky, A. B. 1982. *Risk and Culture: An Essay on the Selection of Technical and Environmental Dangers*. Berkeley, CA: University of California Press.

Drucker, P. F. 1999. *Management Challenges for the 21st Century*. Oxford: Butterworth-Heinemann.

Durance, P. & Godet, M. 2010. Scenario building: Uses and abuses. *Technological Forecasting and Social Change*, 77, 9, 1488–1492.

Ehlert, H., Epkenhans, M. & Gross, G. P. (eds.) 2014. *International Perspectives on the German Strategy for World War 1*. Lexington, KY: University Press of Kentucky.

Eidinow, E. 2007. *Oracles, Curses, and Risk among the Ancient Greeks.* Oxford: Oxford University Press.

Elsbach, K. D., Barr, P. S. & Hargadon, A. B. 2005. Identifying situated cognition in organizations. *Organization Science*, 16, 422–433.

Emory, F. E. & Trist, E. L. 1965. The causal texture of organizational environments. *Human Relations*, 18, 21–32.

Eser, Z., Isin, F. B. & Tolon, M. 2011. Perceptions of marketing academics, neurologists and marketing professionals about neuromarketing. *Journal of Marketing Management*, 27, 854–868.

Fahey, L. R. & Randall, R. M. 1998. *Learning from the Future: Competitive Foresight Scenarios.* New York, NY: Chichester, Wiley.

Fang, T. 1986. *The Chinese View of Life: The Philosophy of Comprehensive Harmony.* Taipei: Linking Publishing Company.

Fisher, R. P. & Geiselman, R. E. 1992. *Memory Enhancing Techniques for Investigative Interviewing: The Cognitive Interview.* Springfield, IL: Charles C. Thomas Books.

Freddosso, A. J. 1988. *Introduction to Luis de Molina.* Ithaca, NY: Cornell University Press.

Galinsky, A. & Moskowitz, G. 2000. Counterfactuals as behavioural primes: Priming the simulation heuristic and consideration of alternatives. *Journal of Experimental Social Psychology*, 36, 384–409.

Geiselman, R. E., Fisher, R. P., MacKinnon, D. P. & Holland, H. L. 1985. Eyewitness memory enhancement in the police interview: Cognitive retrieval mnemonics versus hypnosis. *Journal of Applied Psychology*, 70, 401–412.

Geus, A. D. 1997. *The Living Company: Growth, Learning and Longevity in Business.* London: Nicholas Brealey.

Gilbert, D. T. & Wilson, T. D. 2007. Prospection: Experiencing the future. *Science*, 317, 1351–1354.

Gill, J. & Whittle, S. 1993. Management by panacea: Accounting for intransience. *Journal of Management Studies*, 30, 281–295.

Gioia, D. A. & Chittipeddi, K. 1991. Sensemaking and sensegiving in strategic change initiation. *Strategic Management Journal*, 12, 433–448.

Godet, M. 1982. From forecasting to la 'prospective': A new way of looking at futures. *Journal of Forecasting*, 1, 293–302.

Godet, M. 1987. *Scenarios and Strategic Management.* London: Butterworths.

Godet, M. 1990. Integration of scenarios and strategic management: Using relevant, consistent and likely scenarios. *Futures*, 22, 730–739.

Godet, M. 2001. *Creating Futures: Scenario Planning as a Strategic Management Tool.* London: Economica.

Godet, M. & Roubelat, F. 1996. Creating the future: The use and misuse of scenarios. *Long Range Planning*, 29, 164–171.

Goerlitz, W. 1953. *History of the German General Staff 1657–1945*. New York, NY: Frederick A Praeger.

Goleman, R. D. 1996. *Vital Lies, Simple Truths: The Psychology of Self-Deception*. New York, NY: Simon and Schuster.

Goleman, D. 1998. *Vital Lies, Simple Truths: The Psychology of Self-Deception*. London: Bloomsbury.

Goodwin, P. & Wright, G. 2001. Enhancing strategy evaluation in scenario planning: A role for decision analysis. *Journal of Management Studies*, 38, 1–16.

Gordon, T. J. & Glenn, J. C. 1994. An introduction to the Millennium Project. *Technological Forecasting and Social Change*, 47, 147–170.

Griffith, S. B. 1963. *The Art of War*. Oxford: Oxford University Press.

Grinyer, P. H., Mayes, D. G. & McKiernan, P. 1988. *Sharpbenders: The Secrets of Unleashing Corporate Potential*. Oxford: Basil Blackwell.

Gunn, R. & Williams, W. 2007. Strategic tools: An empirical investigation into strategy in practice in the UK. *Strategic Change*, 16, 201–216.

Hambrick, D. C. & Finkelstein, S. 1995. The effects of ownership structure on conditions at the top: The case of CEO pay rises. *Strategic Management Journal*, 16, 175–193.

Hansson, S. O. 2015. Science and pseudo-science. In Zalta, E. N. (ed.) *The Stanford Encyclopedia of Philosophy*. Stanford, CA: Stanford University Press.

Harries, C. 2003. Correspondence to what? Coherence to what? What is good scenario-based decision making? *Technological Forecasting and Social Change*, 70, 797–817.

Hart-Rudman Commission. 1999. *New World Coming: American Security in the 21st Century*. Washington, DC: US Government Printing Office.

Hartung, A. 2009. *A Key to a Successful Business Plan* [Online]. Available: www.forbes.com/2009/12/07/scenario-planning-strategy-leadership-managing-plan.html#52c68173f20 [Accessed].

Hassabis, D. & Maguire, E. A. 2007. Deconstructing episodic memory with construction. *Trends in Cognitive Sciences*, 11, 299–306.

Hassabis, D., Spreng, R. N., Rusu, A. A., Robbins, C. A., Mar, R. A. & Schacter, D. L. 2013. Imagine all the people: How the brain creates and uses personality models to predict behavior. *Cerebral Cortex*, 24, 299–306.

Helmer, O. 1972. *On the Future State of the Union*. Palo Alto, CA: Institute for the Future.

Hodgkinson, G. P. 1997. The cognitive analysis of competitive structures: A review and critique. *Human Relations*, 50, 625–654.

Hodgkinson, G. & Healy, M. 2008. Toward a (pragmatic) science of strategic intervention: Design propositions for scenario planning. *Organization Studies*, 29, 435–457.

Hodgkinson, G. & Healy, M. 2011. Psychological foundations of dynamic capabilities. *Strategic Management Journal*, 32, 1500–1516.

Hodgkinson, G. P. & Wright, G. 2002. Confronting strategic inertia in a top management team: Learning from failure. *Organization Studies*, 23, 949–977.

Hogarth, R. M. 2001. To what are we trying to generalize? *Behavioural and Brain Sciences*, 24, 416–417.

Huff, A. S. 1982. Industry influences on strategy reformulation. *Strategic Management Journal*, 3, 119–131.

Huizinga, H. 1955. *Homo ludens: A Study of the Play-Element in Culture.* Boston, MA: Bacon Press.

Hume, D. 2007/1748. *An Enquiry Concerning Human Understanding.* Oxford: Oxford University Press.

Huss, W. R. & Honton, E. J. 1987. Scenario planning: What style should you use? *Long Range Planning*, 20, 21–29.

Ingvar, D. H. 1979. Hyperfrontal distribution of the cerebral grey matter flow in resting wakefulness: On the functional anatomy of the conscious state. *Acta Neurologica Scandinavica*, 60, 12–25.

Ingvar, D. H. 1985. Memory of the future: An essay on the temporal organization of conscious awareness. *Human Neurobiology*, 4, 127–136.

Irish, M., Addis, D. R., Hodges, J. R. & Piguet, O. 2012. Considering the role of semantic memory in episodic future thinking: Evidence from semantic dementia. *Brain*, 135, 2178–2191.

James, E. W. & Grim, P. 1982. *On Dismissing Astrology and Other Irrationalities.* Albany, NY: State University of New York Press.

Janis, I. L. 1982. *Groupthink: Psychological Studies of Policy Decisions and Fiascoes.* Boston, MA: Houghton Mifflin.

Janis, I. L. & Mann, L. 1979. *Decision Making: A Psychological Analysis of Conflict, Choice, and Commitment.* New York, NY: Free Press; London: Collier Macmillan.

Janssen, O. 2003. Innovative behaviour and job involvement at the price of conflict and less satisfactory relations with co-workers. *Journal of Occupational and Organizational Psychology*, 76, 347–364.

Janssen, O. 2004. How fairness perceptions make innovative behavior more or less stressful. *Journal of Organizational Behavior*, 25, 201–215.

Jefferson, M. 2012. Shell scenarios: What really happened in the 1970s and what may be learned for current world prospects. *Technological Forecasting and Social Change*, 79, 201–215.

Johnson, G. 1987. *Strategic Change and the Management Process*. Oxford: Basil Blackwell.

Jung, C. G. 1968. *Analytical Psychology: Its Theory and Practice*. London: Routledge & Kegan Paul.

Jung, C. G. 1989. *I Ching or Book of Changes: The Richard Wilhelm Translation*. London: Penguin Books.

Kahn, H. 1960. *On Thermonuclear War*. Princeton, NJ: Princeton University Press.

Kahn, H. 1962. *Thinking about the Unthinkable*. New York, NY: Horizon Press.

Kahn, H. W. & Wiener, A. J. 1967. The next thirty-three years: A framework for speculation. In Bell, D. G. & Graubard, S. R. (eds.) *Toward the Year 2000: Work in Progress*. Cambridge, MA: MIT Press.

Kahneman, D. 2003. A perspective on judgement and choice: Mapping bounded rationality. *American Psychologist*, 58, 697–720.

Kahneman, D., Lovallo, D. & Sibony, O. 2011. Before you make that big decision . . . *Harvard Business Review*, April, 49–53.

Kahneman, D. & Tversky, A. 1973. On the psychology of prediction. *Psychological Review*, 80, 237–251.

Kaplan, S. 2008. Cognition, capabilities and incentives: Assessing firm response to the fibre optic revolution. *Academy of Management Journal*, 51, 672–695.

Kasparov, G. 2005. Strategic intensity: A conversation with world chess champion Garry Kasparov. *Harvard Business Review*, April, 49–53.

Kitchen, M. 1975. *A Military History of Germany from the Eighteenth Century to the Present Day*. London: Weidenfeld and Nicolson.

Klein, H. E., & Linneman, R. K. 1981. The use of scenarios in corporate planning: Eight case histories. *Long Range Planning*, 15, 5, 69–77.

Klein, S. 2013. Making the case that episodic recollection is attributable to operations occurring at retrieval rather than to content stored in a dedicated subsystem of long term memory. *Frontiers in Behavioural Neurology*, 7, 1–14.

Kleiner, A. 1996. *The Age of Heretics: Heroes, Outlaws and the Forerunners of Corporate Change*. London: Nicholas Brealey Publishing.

Koch-Westenholz, U. 1995. *Mesopotamian Astrology*. Copenhagen: Museum Tusculum Press.

Koriat, A., Lichtenstein, S. & Fischhoff, B. 1980. Reasons for confidence. *Journal of Experimental Psychology: Human Learning and Memory* 6, 107–118.

Kosslyn, S. M. & Rosenberg, R. S. 2006. *Psychology in Context*. Boston, MA: Allyn and Bacon.

Kuhn K. M. & Sniezek, J. A. 1996. Confidence and uncertainty in judgmental forecasting: Differential effects of scenario presentation. *Journal of Behavioral Decision Making*, 9, 231–247.

Kuhn, S., Strelow, E. & Gallinat, J. 2016. Multiple 'buy buttons' in the brain: Forecasting chocolate sales at point-of-sale based on functional brain activation using fMRI. *NeuroImage*, 136, 122–128.

Kuhn, T. S. 1970. *Reflections on My Critics: Criticism and the Growth of Knowledge*. Cambridge: Cambridge University Press.

Laing, R. D. 1970. *Knots*. London: Tavistock Publications.

Larrick, R. 2004. Debiasing. In Koehler, D. J. & Harvey, N. (eds.) *Blackwell Handbook of Judgment and Decision Making*. Oxford: Blackwell.

Laureiro-Martinez, D., Brusoni, S., Canessa, N. & Zollo, M. 2015. Understanding the Exploration-Exploitation Dilemma: An fMRI study of attention control and decision-making performance. *Strategic Management Journal*, 36, 319–338.

Levinthal, D. & Rerup, C. 2006. Crossing an apparent chasm: Bridging mindful and less-mindful perspectives on organizational learning. *Organizational Science*, 17, 502–513.

Lindgren, M. & Bandhold, H. 2009. *Scenario Planning: The Link between Future and Strategy*. 2nd edn. Basingstoke: Palgrave Macmillan.

Linneman, R. K. & Klein, H. E. 1983. The use of multiple scenarios by US industrial companies: A comparison study, 1977–1981. *Long Range Planning*, 16, 94–101.

Livingstone, L. P., Nelson, D. L. & Barr, S. H. 1997. Person-environment fit and creativity: An examination of supply-value and demand-ability versions of fit. *Journal of Management*, 23, 119–146.

Lock, A. & Strong, T. 2010. *Social Constructionism: Sources and Stirrings in Theory and Practice*. Cambridge: Cambridge University Press.

Logothetis, N. K. 2008. What we can do and what we cannot do with fMRI. *Nature*, 453, 869–878.

Long, A. A. 2005. Astrology: Arguments pro and contra. In Barbes, J. & Brunschwig, J. (eds.) *Science and Speculation*. Cambridge: Cambridge University Press.

Loveridge, D. 2009. *Foresight: The Art and Science of Anticipating the Future* London: Routledge.

Lusk, J. L., Crespi, J. M., Cherry, J. B. C., McFadden, B. R., Martin, L. E. & Bruce, A. S. 2015. An fMRI investigation of consumer choice regarding controversial food technologies. *Food Quality and Preference*, 40, 209–222.

MacKay, B. & Chia, R. 2013. Choice, chance and unintended consequences in strategic change: A process understanding of the rise and fall of NorthCo automotive. *Academy of Management Journal*, 56, 208–230.

MacKay, B. & McKiernan, P. 2010. Creativity and dysfunction in strategic processes: The case of scenario planning. *Futures*, 42, 271–281.

MacKay, R. B. 2009. Strategic foresight: Counterfactual and prospective sensemaking in enacted environments. In Costanzo, L. A. & MacKay, R. B. (eds.) *Handbook of Research in Strategy and Foresight*. Cheltenham: Edward Elgar.

MacKay, R. & McKiernan, P. 2004. Exploring strategy context with foresight. *European Management Review*, 1, 69–77.

MacKay, R. B. & Stoyanova, V. 2017. Scenario planning with a sociological eye: Augmenting the intuitive logics approach to understanding the future of Scotland and the UK. *Technological Forecasting and Social Change*, 124, 88–100.

Madore, K. P., Gaesser, B. & Schacter, D. L. 2014. Constructive episodic simulation: Dissociable effects of a specificity induction on remembering, imagining and describing in young and older adults. *Journal of Experimental Psychology: Learning, Memory and Cognition*, 40, 609–622.

Makridakis, S. 1990. *Forecasting, Planning and Strategy for the 21st Century*. London: Free Press.

Malaska, P. 1985. Multiple scenario approach and strategic behaviour in European companies. *Strategic Management Journal*, 6, 339–355.

Malaska, P., Malmivirta, M., Meristo, T. & Hansen, S. O. 1984. Scenarios in Europe: Who uses them and why? *Long Range Planning*, 17, 45–49.

Malaska, P. & Virtanen, I. 2005. Theory of futuribles. *Futura*, 2, 10–28.

March, J. G. & Simon, H. A. 1958. *Organizations*. New York, NY: Wiley.

Marcus, A. A. 2009. *Strategic Foresight: A New Look at Scenarios*. Basingstoke: Palgrave Macmillan.

Martelli, A. 2001. Scenario building and scenario planning: State of the art and prospects for evolution. *Futures Research Quarterly*, Summer.

Martin, M. 1988. *The Jesuits: The Society of Jesus and the Betrayal of the Roman Catholic Church*. New York, NY; London: Simon and Schuster,

Mason, D. H. 1994. Scenario-based planning: Decision models for the learning organisation. *Planning Review*, March–April, 7–12.

Masukawa, K. 2016. The origins of board games and ancient board games. In Toshiyuki, K., Hidehiko, K., Yusuke, T. & Paola, R. (eds.) *Simulation and Gaming in the Network Society*. Singapore: Springer.

McClean, C. V. M. 1929. *Babylonian Astrology and Its Relation to the Old Testament*. Toronto: United Church Publishing.

McClure, S. M., Li, J., Tomlin, D., Cypert, K. S., Montague, L. M. & Montague, P. R. 2004. Neural correlates of behavioural preference for culturally familiar drinks. *Neuron*, 44, 379–387.

McGee, J. & Thomas, H. 1986. Strategic groups: Theory, research and taxonomy. *Strategic Management Journal*, 7, 141–160.

McElwee, W. 1974. *The Art of War: Waterloo to Mons*. London: Weidenfeld and Nicolson.

McKiernan, P. 1997. Strategy past; strategy futures. *Long Range Planning*, 30, 790–798.

McKiernan, P. 2008. Scenario planning. In Clegg, S. R. & Bailey, J. R. (eds.) *International Encyclopedia of Organization Studies*. London: Sage.

McKiernan, P. 2017. Prospective thinking: Scenario planning meets neuroscience. *Technological Forecasting and Social Change*, 124, 66–76.

McLelland, V. C., Devitt, A. L., Schacter, D. L. & Addis, D. R. 2015. Making the future memorable: The phenomenology of remembered future events. *Memory*, October, 1–9.

Meissner, P. & Wulf, T. 2013. Cognitive benefits of scenario planning: Its impact on biases and decision quality. *Technological Forecasting and Social Change*, 80, 801–814.

Meri, J. W. 2005. *Medieval Islamic Civilization: An Encyclopedia*. Oxford: Routledge.

Miles, L. K., Christian, B. M., Masilamani, N., Volpi, L. & MacRae, C. N. 2014. Not so close encounters of the third kind: Visual perspective and imagined social interaction. *Social Psychology and Personality Science*, 5, 558–565.

Mill, J. S. 1865. *Auguste Comte and Positivism*. [S.l.] Trubner.

Mill, J. S. 1973/1865. *System of Logic, Ratiocinative and Inductive: Being a Connected View of the Principles of Evidence and the Methods of Scientific Investigation*. Toronto: Toronto University Press.

Miller, D. & Friesen, P. H. 1980. Momentum and revolution in organizational adaptation. *Academy of Management Journal*, 23, 591–614.

Milliken, F. J. 1990. Perceiving and interpreting environmental change: An examination of college administrators' interpretation of changing demographics. *Academy of Management Journal*, 33, 42–63.

Mintzberg, H. 1994. *The Rise and Fall of Strategic Planning*. New York, NY: Free Press.

Mintzberg, H., Ahlstrand, B. & Lampel, J. 2008. *The Strategy Safari: A Tour through the Wilds of Strategic Management*. New York, NY: Free Press.

Miron, E., Erez, M. & Naveh, E. 2004. Do personal characteristics and cultural values that promote innovation, quality, and efficiency compete or complement each other? *Journal of Organizational Behavior*, 25, 175–199.

Mitchell, D. 1980. *The Jesuits: A History*. London: Macdonald.

Murray, H. J. R. 1952. *A History of Board Games Other Than Chess*. Oxford: Clarendon Press.

Nassar, M. R., Rumsey, K. M., Wilson, R. C., Parikh, K., Heasly, B. & Gold, J. I. 2012. Rational regulation of learning dynamics by pupil-linked arousal systems. *Nature Neuroscience*, 15, 1040–1046.

Nassar, M. R., Wilson, R. C., Heasly, B. & Gold, J. I. 2010. An approximately Bayesian delta-rule model explains the dynamics of belief updating in a changing environment. *Journal of Neuroscience*, 30, 12366–12378.

Nickerson, R. S. 1998. Confirmation bias: A ubiquitous phenomenon in many guises. *Review of General Psychology*, 2, 175–190.

O'Brien, F. A. & Meadows, M. 2013. Scenario orientation and use to support strategy development. *Technological Forecasting and Social Change*, 80, 643–656.

O'Brien, F. A., Meadows, M. & Murtland, M. 2007. Creating and using scenarios. In O'Brien, F. A. & Dyson, R. G. (eds.) *Supporting Strategy: Frameworks, Methods and Models*. Chichester: Wiley.

Ocasio, W. 1997. Towards an attention-based view of the firm. *Strategic Management Journal*, 18, 187–206.

Ocasio, W. 2011. Attention to attention. *Organization Science*, 22, 1286–1296.

Ogburn, W. F. 1934. Studies in prediction and the distortion of reality. *Social Forces*, 13, 224–229.

Ogburn, W. F. 1935. Prospecting for the future. *Social Frontier*, 1, 20–22.

Ogburn, W. F. & American Library Association. 1933. *Living with Machines*. Chicago, IL: American Library Association.

Oppenheim, A. L. & Reiner, E. 1977. *Ancient Mesopotamia: Portrait of a Dead Civilization*. Chicago, IL; London: University of Chicago Press.

Pagani, M. 2009. Roadmapping 3G mobile TV: Strategic thinking and scenario planning through repeated cross-impact handling. *Technological Forecasting and Social Change*, 76, 382–395.

Patel, A. 2016. Gaining insight: Re-thinking at the edge. *Technological Forecasting and Social Change*, 107, 141–153.

Phadnis, S., Caplice, C., Sheffi, Y. & Singh, M. Effect of scenario planning on field experts' judgment of long-range investment decisions. *Strategic Management Journal*, 36, 1401–1411.

Pighin, S., Byrne, R. M., Ferrante, D., Gonzelez, M. & Girotto, V. 2011. Counterfactual thoughts about experienced, observed and narrated events. *Thinking & Reasoning*, 17, 197–211.

Poincare, H. 1913. *The Foundations of Science*. Lancaster, PA: Science Press.

Popper, K. 2002/1959. *The Logic of Scientific Discovery*. London: Routledge.

Popper, K. 2004. *Conjectures and Refutations: The Growth of Scientific Knowledge* London: Routledge.

Posner, M. I. & Rothbart, M. K. 2007. Research on attention networks as a model for the integration of psychological science. *Annual Review of Psychology*, 2007, 1–23.

Powell, T. C. 2011. Neuroscience. *Strategic Management Journal*, 32, 1484–1499.

Ramirez, R., Osterman, R. & Gronquist, D. 2013. Scenarios and early warnings as dynamic capabilities to frame managerial attention. *Technological Forecasting and Social Change*, 80, 825–838.

Reisswitz, B. v. 1824. *Instructions for the Representation of Tactical Maneuvers under the Guise of a Wargame*. Berlin.

Reisswitz, B. v. & Leeson, B. 1983. *Kriegsspiel: Instructions for the Representation of Military Manoeuvres with the Kriegsspiel Apparatus*. Hemel Hempstead: B. Leeson.

Rendell, P. G., Bailey, P. E., Henry, J. D., Phillips, L. H., Gaskin, S. & Kliegel, M. 2012. Older adults have greater difficulty imagining future rather than atemporal experiences. *Psychology and Aging*, 27, 1089–1098.

Rigby, D. & Bilodeau, B. 2005. *Management Tools and Trends*. Online. Boston, MA: Bain & Company. Available at www.bain.com/publications/articles/management-tools-and-trends-2015.aspx.

Ringland, G. 2002a. *Scenarios in Public Policy*. Chichester: Wiley.

Ringland, G. 2002b. *Scenarios in Business*. Chichester: Wiley.

Ringland, G., Sparrow, O., & Lustig, P. 2010. *Beyond Crisis: Achieving Renewal in a Turbulent World*. Chichester: Wiley.

Rochberg, F. 2004. *The Heavenly Writing: Divination, Horoscopy and Astronomy in Mesopotamian Culture*. Cambridge: Cambridge University Press.

Rochberg, F. 2013. Foresight in ancient Mesopotamia. In Feller, D. A. (ed.) *Foresight*. Cambridge: Cambridge University Press.

Samples, R. 1976. *The Metaphoric Mind: A Celebration of Creative Consciousness*. Reading: MA, Addison-Wesley.

Sanna, L. J. & Schwarz, N. 2003. Debiasing the hindsight bias: The role of accessibility experiences and (mis)attributions. *Journal of Experimental Social Psychology*, 39, 287–295.

Schacter, D. L. 1999. The Seven Sins of Memory: Insights from psychological and cognitive neuroscience. *American Psychologist*, 54, 182–203.

Schacter, D. L., Benoit, R. G., de Brigard, F. & Szpunar, K. K. 2015. Episodic future thinking and episodic counterfactual thinking: Intersections between memory and decisions. *Neurobiology of Learning and Memory*, 117, 14–21.

Schacter, D. L., Gaesser, B. & Addis, D. R. 2013. Remembering the past and imagining the future in the elderly. *Gerontology*, 59, 143–151.

Schacter, D. L. & Madore, K. P. 2016. Remembering the past and imagining the future: Identifying and enhancing the contribution of episodic memory. *Memory Studies*, 9, 245–255.

Schoemaker, P. J. H. 1991. When and how to use scenario planning – a heuristic approach with illustration. *Journal of Forecasting*, 10, 549–564.

Schoemaker, P. J. H. 1993. Multiple scenario development – its conceptual and behavioral foundation. *Strategic Management Journal*, 14, 193–213.

Schoemaker, P. J. H. 1995. Scenario planning – a tool for strategic thinking. *Sloan Management Review*, 36, 25–40.

Schoemaker, P. J. H. 1997. Disciplined imagination: From scenarios to strategic options. *International Studies of Management and Organization*, 27, 43–70.

Schoemaker, P. J. H. 2004. Forecasting and scenario planning: The challenges of uncertainty and complexity. In Koehler, D. J. & Harvey, N. (eds.) *Blackwell Handbook of Judgment and Decision Making*. Oxford: Blackwell.

Schoemaker, P. J. H. & van der Heijden, C. A. J. M. 1992. Integrating scenarios into strategic planning at Royal Dutch Shell. *Strategy and Leadership*, 20, 41–46.

Schwartz, P. 1991. *The Art of the Long View*. New York, NY: Doubleday/ Currency.

Seidl, D. 2004. The concept of 'weak signals' revisited: A re-description from a constructivist perspective. In Tsoukas, H. & Shepherd, J. (eds.) *Managing the Future: Foresight in the Knowledge Economy*. Oxford: Blackwell.

Seligman, M. R. P., Baumeister, R. & Sripada, C. 2013. Navigating into the future or driven by the past: Prospection as an organizing principle of mind. *Perspectives on Psychological Science*, 8, 119–141.

Selin, C. 2007. Professional dreamers: The future in the past of scenario planning. In Sharpe, B. & van der Heijden., K. (eds.) *Scenarios for Success*. New York, NY: Wiley.

Shotwell, P. 2008. *The Game of Go: Speculations on Its Origins and Symbolism in Ancient China*. Online. New York, NY: American Go Association. Available at www.usgo.org/resources/downloads/originsofgo.pdf.

Simons, D. J. & Chabris, C. F. 1999. Gorillas in our midst: Sustained inattentional blindness for dynamic events. *Perception*, 28, 1059–1074.

Simpson, D. G. 1992. Key lessons for adopting scenario planning in diversified companies. *Planning Review*, 20, 10–17.

Simpson, S. J. 2007. The earliest board games in the Middle East. In Finkel, I. L. E. (ed.) *Ancient Board Games in Perspective*. London: British Museum Press.

Spender, J.-C. 1989. *Industry Recipes: An Enquiry into the Nature and Sources of Managerial Judgement*. Oxford: Wiley-Blackwell.

Steiner, G. A. 1979. *Strategic Planning: What Every Manager Must Know*. New York, NY: Free Press; London: Collier Macmillan.

Stout, D. 1998. Use and abuse of scenarios. *Business Strategy Review*, 9, 2, 27–36.

Suddendorf, T. & Corballis, M. C. 1997. Mental time travel and the evolution of the human mind. *Genetic, Social and General Psychology Monographs*, 123, 133–167.

Suomala, J., Palokangas, L., Leminen, S., Westerlund, M., Heinonen, J. & Numminen, J. 2012. Neuromarketing: Understanding customers' subconscious responses to marketing. *Technology Innovation Management Review*, 2, 12–21.

Sutcliffe, K. M. 1994. What executives notice: Accurate perceptions in top management teams. *Academy of Management Journal*, 37, 1360–1378.

Szpunar, K. K. & Schacter, D. L. 2013. Get real: Effects of repeated simulation and emotion on the perceived plausibility of future experiences. *Journal of Experimental Psychology*, 142, 323.

Szpunar, K. K., Spreng, R. N. & Schacter, D. L. 2014. A taxonomy of prospection: Introducing an organizational framework for future-oriented cognition. *Proceedings of the National Academy of Sciences*, 111, 18414–18421.

Taleb, N. 2007. *The Black Swan*. London: Penguin Books.

Tetlock, P. E. 2005. *Expert Political Judgment*. Princeton, NJ: Princeton University Press.

Thagard, P. R. 1978. Why astrology is a pseudoscience. *PSA: Proceedings of the Biennial Meeting of the Philosophy of Science Association*. JSTOR, 223–234.

Thakral, P. P., Madore, K. P. & Schacter, D. L. 2017. A role for the left angular gyrus in episodic simulation and memory. *Journal of Neuroscience*, 37, 8142–8149.

Tsoukas, H. & Shepherd, J. (eds.) 2004. *Managing the Future: Foresight in the Knowledge Economy*. Oxford: Blackwell.

Tuchman, B. W. 1966. *The Proud Tower: A Portrait of the World before the War, 1890–1914*. London: Hamish Hamilton.

Tucker, P. 2007. The scenario planning handbook: Developing strategies in uncertain times. *Futurist*, 41, 50-50.

Turner, B. 1976. The organizational and interorganizational development of disasters. *Administrative Science Quarterly*, 1, 378–397.

Tversky, A., & Kahneman, D. 1974. Judgement under uncertainty: Heuristics and biases. *Science*, 185, 1124–1134.

Twist, E. 1968. *Future of the Social Sciences*. London: Social Science Research Council.

van der Heijden, K. 1996. *Scenarios: The Art of Strategic Conversation*. Chichester: Wiley.

van der Heijden, K., Bradfield, R., Burt, G., Cairns, G., Wright, G. 2002. *The Sixth Sense: Accelerating Organizational Learning with Scenarios*. Chichester: Wiley.

van Mulukom, V., Schacter, D. L., Corballis, M. C. &Addis, D. R. 2016. The degree of disparateness of event details modulates future simulation construction, plausibility and recall. *Quarterly Journal of Experimental Psychology*, 69, 234–242.

van Klooster, S. A. & van Asselt, M. B. A. 2006. Practicing the Scenario Axis Technique. *Futures*, 38, 15–30.

van Vught, F. A. 1987. Pitfalls of forecasting: Fundamental problems for the methodology of forecasting from the philosophy of science. *Futures*, 19, 184–196.

Varum, C. & Melo, C. 2010. Directions in scenario planning literature – a review of the past decades. *Futures*, 42, 355–369.

Volkov, Y. G. 2016. Scenario thinking in the context of sociological diagnostics. *Sotsiologicheskie Issledovaniya*, 13.

von Hilgers, P. 2012. *War Games: A History of War on Paper*. Cambridge, MA: MIT Press.

von Karman, T. 1945. *Towards New Horizons*. Los Angeles, CA: Army Air Force Scientific Advisory Group.

Wack, P. 1985a. Unchartered waters ahead. *Harvard Business Review*, September–October 73–89.

Wack, P. 1985b. Scenarios: Shooting the rapids. *Harvard Business Review*, November–December, 139–150.

Walsh, J. P. 1995. Managerial and organizational cognition: Notes from a trip down memory lane. *Organization Science*, 6, 280–321.

Warren, C. M. & Holroyd, C. B. 2012. The impact of deliberative strategy dissociates ERP components related to conflict processing vs. reinforcement learning. *Frontiers in Neuroscience*, 6, 1–17.

Warren, C. M., Murphy, P. R. & Nieuwenhuis, S. 2016. Cognitive control, dynamic salience and the imperative toward computational accounts of neuromodulatory function. *Behavioral and Brain Sciences*, 39.

on, M. & Bazerman, M. 2003. Predictable surprises: The disasters you should have seen coming, and how to prevent them. *Harvard Business Review*, 81, 72–80.

Weisberg, R. W. 1993. *Beyond the Myth of Genius*. New York, NY: Freeman.

Wells, H. G. 1932 (1987). Wanted: Professors of foresight! *Futures Research Quarterly*, 3, 89–91.

Whittington, R. 2006. Completing the practice turn in strategy research. *Organization Studies*, 27, 613–634.

Wilensky, H. L. 1967. *Organizational Intelligence*. New York, NY: Basic Books.

Wilkinson, A. 2009. Scenarios practices: in search of theory. *Journal of Futures Studies*, 13, 107–114.

Wilkinson, A. & Kupers, R. 2014. *The Essence of Scenarios: Learning from the Shell Experience*. Amsterdam: Amsterdam University Press.

Willmore, J. 2001. Scenario planning: Creating strategy for uncertain times. *Information Outlook*, 5, 23–39

Wilson, I. 2000. From scenario thinking to strategic action. *Technological Forecasting and Social Change*, 65, 23–29.

Wiltbank, R., Dew, N., Read, S. & Sarasvthy, S. 2006. What to do next? The case for non predictive strategy. *Strategic Management Journal*, 27, 981–998.

Wolf, R. C., Carpenter, R. W., Warren, C. M., Zeier, J. D., Baskin-Sommers, A. R. & Newman, J. P. 2011. Reduced susceptibility to the attentional blink in psychopathic offenders: Implications for the attentional bottleneck hypothesis. *Neuropsychology*, 26, 102–109.

Wood, C. 1970. *Chaucer and the Country of the Stars: Poetical Uses of Astrological Imagery*. Princeton, NJ: Princeton University Press.

Wright, G., Bradfield, R., & Cairns, G. 2013. Does the intuitive logics method – and its recent enhancements – produce effective scenarios? *Technological Forecasting and Social Change*, 80, 631–642.

Wright, G. & Cairns, G. 2011. *Scenario Thinking: Practical Approaches to the Future*. Basingstoke: Palgrave Macmillan.

Wright, G., Cairns, G. & Goodwin, P. 2009. Teaching scenario planning: Lessons from practice in academe and business. *European Journal of Operational Research*, 194, 323–335.

Wright, G. & Goodwin, P. 2002. Eliminating a framing bias by using simple instructions to 'think harder' and respondents with managerial experience: Comment on 'breaking the frame'. *Strategic Management Journal*, 23, 1059–1067.

Wright, G. & Goodwin, P. 2009. Decision making and planning under low levels of predictability: Enhancing the scenario method. *International Journal of Forecasting*, 25, 813–825.

Wright, G., van der Heijden, K., Burt, G., Bradfield, R. & Cairns, G. 2008. Scenario planning interventions in organizations: An analysis of the causes of success and failure. *Futures*, 40, 218–236.

Wyman, A. J. & Vyse, S. 2008. Science versus the stars: A double-blind test of the validity of the NEO five-factor inventory and computer-generated astrological natal charts. *Journal of General Psychology*, 135, 287–300.

Young, M. D. 1958. *The Rise of the Meritocracy, 1870-2033: An Essay on Education and Equality*. London: Thames & Hudson.

Zajac, E. & Bazerman, M. 1991. Blind spots in industry and competitor analysis: Implications of interfirm (mis)perceptions for strategic decisions. *Academy of Management Review*, 16, 37–56.

Zhou, J. & George, J. M. 2001. When job dissatisfaction leads to creativity: Encouraging the expression of voice. *Academy of Management Journal*, 44, 682–696.

Zuber, T. 2004. *German War Planning, 1891–1914: Sources and Interpretations*. Woodbridge and Rochester, NY: Boydell Press.

Cambridge Elements ≡

Business Strategy

J.-C. Spender

Rutgers Business School

J.-C. Spender is a visiting scholar at Rutgers Business School and a research professor at Kozminski University. He has been active in the business strategy field since 1971 and is the author or coauthor of seven books and numerous papers. His principal academic interest is in knowledge-based theories of private sector firms and how to manage them.

About the Series

Business strategy's reach is vast, and important too, since wherever there is business activity, there is strategizing. As a field, strategy has a long history from medieval and colonial times to today's developed and developing economies. This series offers a place for interesting and illuminating research, including industry and corporate studies, strategizing in service industries, the arts, the public sector, and the new forms of Internet-based commerce. It also covers today's expanding gamut of analytic techniques.

Cambridge Elements ≡

Business Strategy

Elements in the Series

Made in the USA
Columbia, SC
24 August 2020